Leadership: A Very Short Introduction

Very Short Introductions available now:

For more information visit our website

www.oup.co.uk/general/vsi/

Keith Grint

LEADERSHIP

A Very Short Introduction

OXFORD
UNIVERSITY PRESS

OXFORD
UNIVERSITY PRESS

Great Clarendon Street, Oxford OX2 6DP

Oxford University Press is a department of the University of Oxford.
It furthers the University's objective of excellence in research, scholarship,
and education by publishing worldwide in

Oxford New York

Auckland Cape Town Dar es Salaam Hong Kong Karachi
Kuala Lumpur Madrid Melbourne Mexico City Nairobi
New Delhi Shanghai Taipei Toronto

With offices in

Argentina Austria Brazil Chile Czech Republic France Greece
Guatemala Hungary Italy Japan Poland Portugal Singapore
South Korea Switzerland Thailand Turkey Ukraine Vietnam

Oxford is a registered trade mark of Oxford University Press
in the UK and in certain other countries

Published in the United States
by Oxford University Press Inc., New York

First published 2010

British Library Cataloguing in Publication Data

Data available

Library of Congress Cataloging in Publication Data

Data available

Typeset by SPI Publisher Services, Pondicherry, India
Printed in Great Britain by
Ashford Colour Press Ltd, Gosport, Hampshire

ISBN 978-0-19-956991-5

1 3 5 7 9 10 8 6 4 2

Contents

Acknowledgements

This little book is the culmination of a very large number of conversations with many friends, colleagues, and students over more than twenty years. Amongst those, I would like to thank the following: John Antonakis, John Atkinson, Richard Badham, John Benington, David Bolger, John Bratton, Stephen Brookes, Alan Bryman, Brigid Carroll, Peter Case, Andy Coleman, David Collinson, Rhys Cowsill, Rebecca Cox, Sue Dopson, Mike Dunn, Gareth Edwards, Paul Ellis, Gail Fairhurst, Yiannis Gabriel, Amanda Giles, Jonathan Gosling, David Grant, Peter Gray, Mike Harper, Jean Hartley, Julia Hockey, Richard Holmes, Kerry Iwaniszyn, Brad Jackson, Kim James, Doris Jepson, Drew Jones, Owain Jones, John Jupp, Andrew Kakabadse, Mihaela Kelemen, Nannerl Keohane, Donna Ladkin, Boje Larsen, Jim Lawless, Patrick Leonard, Sarah Lewis, James McCalman, Kevin Morrell, Anne Murphy, Janine Nahapiet, Debra Nelson, Hilarie Owen, Ken Parry, Edward Peck, Gillian Peele, Lesley Prince, Tracy Reeves, Robin Ryde, Jim Scholes, Boas Shamir, Joe Simpson, David Sims, Amanda Sinclair, Georgia Sorenson, Gillian Stamp, Mark Stein, John Storey, Stefan Sveningsson, Marc Thompson, Dennis Tourish, Irwin Turbitt, Linda Sue Warner, Holly Wheeler, Martin Wood, Steve Woolgar, and Marshall Young. I would also like to thank the anonymous reviewers, especially the final reviewer. Finally, I would like to thank my family for everything else: Adam, Beki, Katy, Kris, Rebecca, Richie, and, of course, Sandra.

List of illustrations

Chapter 1
What is leadership?

Introduction

What is leadership? Well, despite almost three thousand years of ponderings and over a century of 'academic' research into leadership, we appear to be no nearer a consensus as to its basic meaning, let alone whether it can be taught or its effects measured and predicted. This cannot be because of a dearth of interest or material: on 29 October 2003, there were 14,139 books relating to 'leadership' on Amazon.co.uk for sale. Just over six years later, that number had almost quadrupled to 53,121 – and clear evidence that within a short space of time there will be more books about leadership than people to read them. You would be forgiven for thinking that more information equates to greater understanding. Unfortunately, we just seem to generate ever-greater disparity in our understandings and seem no nearer 'the truth' about defining leadership than before we began to publish so much material. Indeed, my own journey through the literature is represented in Figure 1. When I began reading the leadership literature in about 1986, I had already spent some time in various leadership positions, so at that time I'd read little but I understood everything about the subject from the University of Life. Then, as I read more material, I realized that all my previous 'truths' were built on very dubious foundations, so my understanding decreased as my knowledge increased. 2006 was a difficult year: I'd read hundreds,

1

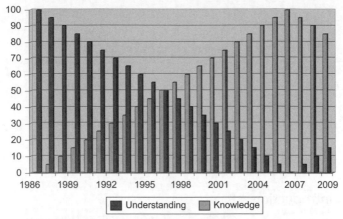

1. Leadership: knowledge and understanding

if not thousands, of books and articles, and concluded that Socrates was right – wisdom only comes when you realize how ignorant you are. I think I'm now on the road to recovery and have got past base camp with this conclusion: at its most basic, the 'essence' of leadership – as an individual leader – leaves out the followers, and without followers you cannot be a leader. Indeed, this might be the simplest definition of leadership: 'having followers'.

So how are we going to approach this topic? The importance of the definition of leadership is not simply to delineate a space in a language game, and it is not merely a game of sophistry; indeed, we don't need to agree on the definition (though organizations probably should), but we should at least be able to understand each other's position so as to make sense of each other's arguments. After all, how we define leadership has vital implications for how organizations work – or don't work – who we reward and punish. Over 50 years ago, W. B. Gallie called power an 'essentially contested concept' (ECC). Gallie suggested that many concepts – such as power – involved 'endless disputes about their proper uses on the part of the users', to the point where debates appeared irresolvable. For example, a discussion about whether Bush or

Blair were 'good' leaders is likely to generate more heat than light, and precious little hope of a consensus amongst people who bring different definitions of 'good' leadership to the debate.

So we don't need to agree on the definition, but we need to know what the definitions are. We might start by considering what the most popular books have to say on the issue. Many are based on autobiographical or biographical accounts – they relate leadership to the *person* regarded as the leader. Others define leadership as a *process* – this may be the style that leaders adopt, or a process such as 'sense-making' (according to Weick, 'the process by which information which is undigested and contradictory is made sense of'), or the practices of leaders. Some define leadership by simply considering what those in authority do – a *positional* approach. Often, the definition is close to that of power, drawn from Weber's and Dahl's original idea that power (and thus leadership) was the ability to get someone to do something they wouldn't otherwise have done. This approach tends to lock leadership into mobilizing a group or community to achieve a purpose – a *results* approach. Some of these we shall return to, but, apart from noting the varying properties of these definitions, we are left more, rather than less, confused by them. Leadership does seem to be defined differently and, even if there are some similarities, the complexities undermine most attempts to explain why the differences exist. However, the dissensus seems to hang around four areas of dispute, leadership defined as *position* or *person* or *result* or *process*.

This fourfold typology does not claim universal coverage, but it should encompass a significant proportion of our definitions of leadership. Moreover, the typology is not hierarchical: it does not claim that one definition is more important than another and, contrary to the consensual approach, it is constructed upon foundations that *may* be mutually exclusive. In effect, we may have to choose which form of leadership we are talking about rather than attempt to elide the differences. It is, however, quite possible that empirical examples of leadership embody elements of all four forms. Thus we are left with four major alternatives:

- Leadership as *position*: is it *where* 'leaders' operate that makes them leaders?
- Leadership as *person*: is it *who* 'leaders' are that makes them leaders?
- Leadership as *result*: is it *what* 'leaders' achieve that makes them leaders?
- Leadership as *process*: is it *how* 'leaders' get things done that makes them leaders?

All these aspects are 'ideal types', following Weber's assertion that no such 'real' empirical case probably exists in any pure form, but this does enable us to understand the phenomenon of leadership better – and its attendant confusions and complexities – because leadership means different things to different people. This is therefore a heuristic model – a pragmatic attempt to make sense of the world – not an attempt to carve up the world into 'objective' segments that mirror what we take to be reality. I will suggest, having examined these four different approaches to leadership, that the differences explain both why so little agreement has been reached on the definition of leadership and why this is important to the execution and analysis of leadership.

Defining leadership

Position-based leadership

Leadership is traditionally related to a spatial position in an organization of some kind – formal or informal. Thus we can define leadership as the activity undertaken by someone whose position on a vertical, and usually formal, hierarchy provides them with the resources to lead. These people are 'above us', 'at the top of the tree', 'superordinates', and so on. In effect, they exhibit what we might call 'leadership-in-charge'. This is how we normally perceive the heads of vertical hierarchies, whether CEOs or military generals or head teachers or their equivalents. These people lead from their positional control over large networks of subordinates and tend to drive any required change from the top. That 'drive' also hints at both the mechanistic assumptions about how organizations work and the coercion that is available to those in charge: a general can order executions, a judge can imprison people, and a CEO can discipline or sack employees, and so on.

A related aspect of this vertical structuring is what appears to be the parallel structuring of power and responsibility. Since the leader is 'in charge', then presumably he or she can ensure the enactment of his or her will. But while a formal leader may *demand* obedience from his or her subordinates – and normally acquire it, among other things, because of the resource imbalance – that obedience is never guaranteed. In fact, one could suggest that power encompasses a counterfactual possibility, a subjunctivist verb tense rather than just a verb – it could have been otherwise. Indeed, one could well argue that power is not so much a cause of subordinate action as a consequence of it: if subordinates do as leaders demand, then, and only then, are leaders powerful. If this was not the case, then we could not explain a mutiny – an act of insubordination in a military hierarchy that can occur only if the subordinate has the power to say 'no' – and the courage to face the consequences.

The limitations of restricting leadership to a position within a vertical hierarchy are also exposed when we move to consider leadership-in-front, a horizontal approach, in which leadership is largely unrelated to vertical hierarchies and is usually informally constituted through a network or a heterarchy (a flexible and fluid hierarchy). Leadership 'in-front' might be manifest in several forms, and where it merges into leadership-in-charge might be at the penultimate rank at the bottom of a hierarchy. For instance, within an army such leadership might be manifest in corporals who have some degree of formal authority but may secure their position with the ordinary soldiers – their followers – through leading from the front. Indeed, the leadership abilities of low-level leaders may be critical in differentiating the success of armies. It may be, for example, that the old adage about sergeants being 'the backbone of the army' has more than a trace of truth in it.

More commonly, though, we might conceive of leadership-in-front from a fashion leader – someone who is 'in front' of his or her followers, whether that is trends in clothing, music, culture, business models, or whatever. These leaders provide guides to the mass of fashion-followers without any formal authority over them. But leading from the front also encompasses those who guide others, either a professional guide showing the way or simply whoever knows the best way to an agreed destination amongst a group of friends on a Sunday stroll; both guides exhibit leadership through their role in front but neither is necessarily formally instituted into an official hierarchy. We might even retrace the origins of the English word for leadership to shed light on this aspect. The etymological roots of the English word 'leadership' derive from the Old German '*Lidan*', to go; the Old English '*Lithan*', to travel; and the Old Norse '*Leid*', to find the way at sea.

Leadership-in-front might also be provided in the sense of legitimizing otherwise prohibited behaviour. For instance, we might consider how Hitler's overt and public anti-Semitism legitimated the articulation of anti-Semitism by his followers. And again it has been suggested that acts such as suicide or antisocial behaviour such as graffiti provide 'permission' by 'leaders-in-front' for others to follow, hence there are often spates of similar acts in quick succession, almost as if the social behaviour operates as an epidemic.

Leadership along this positional dimension, then, differs according to the extent to which it is formally or informally structured, and vertically or horizontally constituted. Leadership-in-charge implies some degree of centralizing resources and authority, while leadership-in-front might, in some circumstances, imply something closer to leading without authority. But does this imply that the character of the leader is less relevant than where that leader operates from?

Person-based leadership

Is it who you are that determines whether you are a leader or not? This, of course, resonates with the traditional traits approach: a leader's character or personality. We might consider the best example of this as the charismatic to whom followers are attracted because of the charismatic's personal 'magnetism'. Ironically, while a huge effort has been made to reduce the ideal leader to his or her essence – the quintessential characteristics or competencies or behaviours of the leader – the effort of reduction has simultaneously reduced its value. It is rather as if a leadership scientist had turned chef and was engaged in reducing a renowned leader to his or her elements by placing them in a saucepan and applying heat. Eventually the residue left from the cooking could be analysed and the material substances divided into their various chemical compounds. But, although it may be that some chemical residues do, paradoxically, have exactly this ability (heroin, for example, is often blamed for 'leading' people astray), the question 'what is leadership?' is unanswerable because it is not possible to analyse leaders in the absence of followers or contexts.

A complementary or contradictory case can also be made for defining leadership generally as a collective, rather than an individual, phenomenon. In this case, the focus usually moves from an individual formal leader to multiple informal leaders. We might, for example, consider how organizations actually achieve anything, rather than being over-concerned with what the CEO has said should be achieved. Thus we could trace the role of informal opinion-leaders in persuading their colleagues to work differently, or to work harder, or not to work at all, and so on. We shall return to this issue in Chapter 7.

Either way, leadership along this criterion is primarily defined by *who* the leader is or leaders are (formal and informal), and it may be that such an approach is associated with an emotional relationship between leader and followers or between leaders. At its most extreme, this emotional relationship renders the followers in 'the crowd' incapable of discriminating between good and bad actions.

Despite the Western fetish for heroic individuals as leadership icons, it is not at all clear that such examples exist in social isolation. For instance, Newton may claim to have 'led' the discovery of gravity, but it was, in effect, the result of collective work by Robert Hooke and Edmund Halley as well as Newton. We might also want to differentiate here between leadership as means and ends. For instance, the assembly line is the *means* by which workers are 'led' to act. But the *ends* do not originate in the machinery; instead, they are constructed by the present but invisible human leader(s). So how important are the ends – the results – of leadership?

Results-based leadership

It might be more appropriate to take the results-based approach because without results – the purpose of leadership – there is little support for it. There may be thousands of individuals who are 'potentially' great leaders, but if that potential is never realized, if no products of that leadership are forthcoming, then it would be logically difficult to speak of these people as 'leaders', except in the sense of 'failed' or 'theoretical' leaders – people who actually achieve little or nothing. On the other hand, there is a tendency to focus on results as both the primary criterion for leadership and as attributed to leaders: for example, since the company achieved a 200% increase in profits – which is its primary purpose – we should reward the leader appropriately. But there are two other issues that need further examination here. First, why and how do we attribute the collective products of an organization to the actions of the individual leader? Second, assuming that we can causally link the two, do the methods by which the products are achieved play any role in determining the presence of leadership?

The first issue – that we can trace effects back to the actions of individual leaders – is deeply controversial. On the one hand, there are several studies from a psychological approach that suggest it is possible to measure the effect of leaders, but more sociologically inclined authors often deny the validity of such measures. Thus we may have clear evidence of success – or failure – and we know who the leader was at the time, but we are rarely in a position to say, categorically, that the actions of the leader led directly to the results (see Rosenzweig on this issue, listed in the further reading section). More often, there are a whole raft of people and processes involved that separate the leader from the result. Why, then, you might ask, do we typically focus on the leader for responsibility? Émile Durkheim, a French sociologist writing at the end of the 19th and beginning of the 20th centuries, argued that followers actually wanted their leaders to be god-like in their powers. This served the followers in two separate but related ways: first, all the responsibility for difficult decisions could be placed on the leader (thereby justifying the significant disparity in rewards given to leaders and followers); second, when (rather than if) that leader failed, the followers would scapegoat him or her and thus cleanse themselves of any responsibility. The most extreme case against results-based leadership, especially the results of 'Great Men', is made by Tolstoy in *War and Peace*, in which he likens leaders to bow waves of moving boats – always in front and theoretically leading, but, in practice, not leading but merely being pushed along by the boat (organization) itself.

This brings us to the second issue at the heart of results-based leadership – does the process by which the results are achieved actually matter? Most certainly, the office or school bully who successfully 'encourages' followers to comply under threat of punishment becomes a leader under the results-based criteria – providing they are successful in their coercion and its effects. But such a results-based approach to leadership immediately sets it at odds with some perspectives that differentiate leaders according to some putative distinction between leadership – which is allegedly non-coercive – and all other forms of activity that we might regard as the actions of a 'bully' or a 'tyrant' and so on. Indeed, most aspects of leadership use motivational strategies that can be regarded by some people – especially those subject to them – as coercive. Thus a religious charismatic might regard his or her actions as simply based on revealing the truth to their followers – who are then free to choose to follow or not as they wish. But if the followers believe that failure to adhere to religious principles will lead to eternal damnation and a slow roast in hell, then they might consider that as coercive. Equally, an employer may not regard an employment contract as coercive since both parties freely enter into it, but if the employee feels that failing to work at the requisite level will lead to 'the sack' – with all its attendant embarrassment, discrimination, and penury – then he or she may believe the contract to be coercive. Nevertheless, for those who perceive leadership to be primarily purposive, focused on results, the process by which these results were obtained, or even whether the leader was responsible for them, may be insignificant.

Of course, results-based leadership need not be restricted to authoritarian or unethical leaders; on the contrary, it can also be exemplified by eminently practical people who may be distinctly uncharismatic but very effective in getting things done. Much of their work may often go unnoticed, but it may also be critical in keeping the organization moving, and this form of leadership may be associated with an appeal to the interests of followers rather than their emotional relationships.

One particularly well-supported case of this is that of Benjamin Franklin, whose early successes seem not to have been based on articulating a compelling vision or rousing the emotions of followers to transcend their personal interests in favour of the greater good. On the contrary, Franklin's pragmatic leadership was rooted in finding practical solutions to outstanding problems that engaged the interests, rather than the emotions, of others. Yet those mobilized by Franklin were not simply involved in an exchange process with him, as understood in transactional theories of leadership, because, for example, in instigating the development in Philadelphia of a police force, a hospital, a paper currency, paving, lighting, and volunteer fire departments, and so on, Franklin's skill lay in persuading his colleagues to solve their own practical problems. An important point here is the visibility of Franklin's leadership, for although the results were clear, the hand that secured the results was not. In effect, if Franklin had died early in his career, it may well be that much of this backroom networking may not have become apparent and that he would not have been considered a great leader.

Thus results-based leadership can embody both highly visible charismatic individuals and almost completely invisible 'social engineers'; moreover, it contains approaches that can range from 'what have we achieved', in terms of targets reached, goals secured, and so on, to 'what are we here for?' – a purposive or identity-focused philosophy to which we shall return. But, as I suggested above, not everyone accepts that the most important issue is the results, rather the methods; so does focusing upon the processes by which leadership is recognized offer a radically different perspective?

Process-based leadership

There is an assumption that people to whom we attribute the term 'leader' act differently from non-leaders – that some people 'act like leaders' – but what does this mean? It could mean that the context is critical, or that leaders must be exemplary, or that the attribution of difference starts early in the lives of individuals such that 'natural' leaders can be perceived in the school playgrounds or on the sports field. But what is this 'process' differential? Are leaders those who allegedly embody the exemplary performance we require to avoid any hint of hypocrisy?

And when sacrifice is required or new forms of behaviour demanded from followers, is it exemplary leaders who are the most successful?

Perhaps, but think of two counter-examples that contradict this ideal type. First, sergeant majors tend to secure followers whether they embody exemplary action or not. We might argue that coercive sergeant majors who scream at recruits on the parade ground are not 'really' leaders, but if their leadership processes do indeed produce trained soldiers, are we to deduce that the military, because it is rooted in coercive mechanisms, cannot demonstrate leadership? Or is it that what counts as a legitimate leadership process depends upon the local culture? That is, soldiers expect to be coerced, and would probably not recognize attempts by their sergeants or officers to reach a consensus by egalitarian debate as 'leadership'?

The second counter-example is Admiral Nelson, an individual whose military successes were almost always grounded in a paradoxical situation wherein he demanded absolute obedience from his subordinates to naval regulations but who personally broke just about every rule in that same rule book. Yet Nelson's success was not simply a consequence of rule-breaking actions but also a result of his engagement with, and motivation of, his followers, most importantly his fellow officers in his battle fleet, his 'Band of Brothers'. Hence, at one level, this process approach may encompass the specific skills and resources that motivate followers: rhetoric, coercion, bribery, exemplary behaviour, bravery, and so on. Leadership under this guise is necessarily a relational concept, not a possessional one. In other words, it does not matter whether you think you have great process skills if your followers disagree with you. Thus it may be that we can recognize leadership by the behavioural processes that differentiate leaders from followers, but this does not mean we can simply list the processes as universally valid across space and time. After all, we would not expect a 2nd-century Roman leader to act in the same way as a

21st-century Italian politician (though they might), yet it remains the case that most of our assumptions about leadership relate to our own cultural context rather than someone else's – a Pandora's box of complexity that is beyond this small introduction (see Chhokar et al., in the further reading section).

Indeed, while many accounts of the leadership process might focus upon the acts of 'Great Men', it has long been a point of great controversy as to whether men and women lead in the same way or in ways that are genetically or culturally influenced by their genders. And while Thomas Carlyle's heroic 'men' *solve* the problems of their followers (see Chapters 3 and 4), it may be that leadership is really related to making followers face up to their own responsibilities. Indeed, it may be that leadership – for most people – has little to do with any form of heroics and is rather a consequence of much more 'mundane' and everyday practices through which social relationships and thus social capital are built and strengthened, though the label 'mundane' underestimates the skill and precision required to perform these intricate acts, for they are meticulously constructed. Indeed, to those of us unable to reproduce such acts, they appear more like the tacit skills of a magician – ostensibly simple but impossible to explain. Thus it is the assiduous leaders who, for example, consistently ask about the health of their followers' families, or who always make a point of ensuring their followers are in agreement with the direction of the organization and their work rate, who build the networks that make the organization work.

It is, therefore, not how many leadership competences you can tick off on your CV that makes you a successful leader, for these are inevitably decontextualized. What, for instance, is the point of having a high level of competence in public speaking when your leadership is required in a place where no public speaking role is required? Competences, then, are often essentially related to an individual – yet leadership is necessarily a relational phenomenon: without followers, you cannot be a leader, no matter how many 'individual' competences you might have. Instead, we might consider the importance of leadership 'practices' – not what leaders 'have', but what they 'do'. But do leaders also engage in activities that may not be regarded as leadership? This is the focus of the next chapter.

Chapter 2
What isn't leadership?

If, as Chapter 1 suggested, we probably have markedly different definitions of leadership, how might we differentiate leadership from management? This chapter poses one way of doing this. Much of the writing in the field of leadership research is grounded in a typology that distinguishes between leadership and management as different forms of authority – that is, legitimate power – with leadership tending to embody longer time periods, a more strategic perspective, and a requirement to resolve novel problems. Another way to put this is that the division is rooted partly in the context: management is the equivalent of *déjà vu* (seen this before), whereas leadership is the equivalent of *vu jàdé* (never seen this before). If this is valid, when acting as a manager, you are required to engage the requisite process – the standard operating procedure (SOP) – to resolve the previously experienced problem the last time it emerged. In contrast, when you are acting as a leader, you are required to facilitate the construction of an innovative response to the novel or recalcitrant problem.

Management and leadership, as two forms of authority rooted in the distinction between certainty and uncertainty, can also be related to Rittell and Webber's typology of 'tame' and 'wicked' problems. A tame problem may be complicated but is resolvable through unilinear acts, and it is likely to have occurred before. In other words, there is only a limited degree of uncertainty, and thus it is associated with management. Tame problems are akin to puzzles – for which there is always an answer. The (scientific) manager's role, therefore, is to provide the appropriate process to solve the problem. Examples would include timetabling the railways, building a nuclear plant, training in the army, or planned heart surgery.

A wicked problem is complex, rather than just complicated – that is, it cannot be removed from its environment, solved, and returned without affecting the environment. Moreover, there is no clear relationship between cause and effect. Such problems are often intractable. For instance, trying to develop a National Health Service (NHS) on the basis of a scientific approach (assuming it was a tame problem) would suggest providing everyone with all the services and medicines they required based only on their medical needs. However, with an ageing population, an increasing medical ability to intervene and maintain life, and a decreasing financial resource to fund such intervention, we have a potentially infinite increase in demand but a finite level of economic resource, so there cannot be a scientific or medical, or tame, solution to the problem of the NHS. In sum, we cannot provide everything for everybody; at some point, we need to make a political decision about who gets what and based on which criteria. This inherently contested arena is typical of a wicked problem. If we think about the NHS as the 'NIS' – the National Illness Service – then we have a different understanding of the problem because it is essentially a series of tame problems: fixing a broken leg is the equivalent of a tame problem – there is a scientific solution and medical professionals in hospitals know how to fix it. But if you run (sorry, crawl) into a restaurant for your broken leg to be fixed, it becomes a wicked problem because it's unlikely that anyone there will have the knowledge or the resources to fix it. Thus the category of problems is subjective not objective – what kind of a problem you have depends on where you are and what you already know.

Moreover, many of the problems that the NHS deals with – obesity, drug abuse, violence – are not simply problems of health, they are often deeply complex social problems that sit across and between different government departments and institutions, so attempts to treat them through a single institutional framework are almost bound to fail. Indeed, because there is often no 'stopping point' with wicked problems – that is, the point at which the problem is solved (for example, there will be no more crime because we have solved it) – we often end up having to admit that we cannot solve wicked problems. Conventionally, we associate leadership with precisely the opposite – the ability to solve problems, act decisively, and to know what to do. But we cannot know how to solve wicked problems, and therefore we need to be very wary of acting decisively precisely because we cannot know what to do. If we knew what to do, it would be a tame problem not a wicked problem. Yet the pressure to act decisively often leads us to try to solve the problem as if it were a tame problem. When global warming first emerged as a problem, some of the responses concentrated on solving the problem through science (a tame response), manifest in the development of biofuels; but we now know that the first generation of biofuels appear to have denuded the world of significant food resources, so that what looked like a solution actually became another problem. Again, this is typical of what happens when we try to solve wicked problems – other problems emerge to compound the original problem. So we can make things better or worse – we can drive our cars slower and less or faster and more – but we may not be able to solve global warming, we may just have to learn to live with a different world and make the best of it we can. In other words, we cannot start again and design a perfect future – though many political and religious extremists might want us to.

The 'we' in this is important because it signifies the importance of the collective in addressing wicked problems. Tame problems might have individual solutions in the sense that individuals are likely to know how to deal with them. But since wicked problems are partly defined by the absence of an answer on the part of the leader, then it behoves the individual leader to ask the right kind of questions to engage the collective in an attempt to come to terms with the problem. In other words, wicked problems require the transfer of authority from individual to collective because only collective engagement can hope to address the problem. The uncertainty involved in wicked problems implies that leadership, as I am defining it, is not a science but an art – the art of engaging a community in facing up to complex collective problems.

Examples of wicked problems would include developing a transport strategy, or a response to global warming, or a response to antisocial behaviour, or a national health system. Wicked problems are not necessarily rooted in longer time frames than tame problems, because often an issue that appears to be tame can be turned into a (temporary) wicked problem by delaying the decision. For example, President Kennedy's actions during the Cuban Missile Crisis were often based on asking questions of his civilian assistants that required some time for reflection – despite the pressure from his military advisers to provide instant answers. Had Kennedy accepted the advice of the American Hawks, we would have seen a third set of problems that fall outside the wicked/tame dichotomy – a 'critical' problem, in this case probably a nuclear war.

A critical problem, that is, a crisis, is presented as self-evident in nature, as encapsulating very little time for decision-making and action, and it is often associated with authoritarianism. Here there is virtually no uncertainty about what needs to be done, at least in the behaviour of the commander, whose role is to take the required decisive action – that is, to provide the answer to the problem, not to engage SOPs (management) if these delay the decision, or ask questions and seek collaborative assistance (leadership).

Translated into critical problems, I suggest that for such crises we do need decision-makers who are god-like in their decisiveness and their ability to provide the answer to the crisis. And since we reward people who are good in crises (and ignore people who are such good managers that there are very few crises), commanders soon learn to seek out (or reframe situations as) crises. Of course, it may be that the commander remains privately uncertain about whether the action is appropriate or the presentation of the situation as a crisis is persuasive, but that uncertainty will probably not be apparent to the followers of the commander. Examples would include the immediate response to a major train crash, a leak of radioactivity from a nuclear plant, a military onslaught, a heart attack, an industrial strike, the loss of employment or a loved one, or a terrorist attack such as 9/11 or the 7 July bombings in London.

These three forms of authority – command, management, and leadership – are, in turn, another way of suggesting that the role of those responsible for decision-making is to find the appropriate answer, process, and question to address the problem, respectively. This is not meant as a discrete typology but an heuristic device to enable us to understand why those charged with decision-making sometimes appear to act in ways that others find incomprehensible. Thus, I am not suggesting that the correct decision-making process lies in the correct analysis of the situation – that would be to generate a deterministic approach – but I am suggesting that decision-makers tend to legitimize their actions on the basis of a persuasive account of the situation. In short, the social construction of the problem legitimizes the deployment of a particular form of authority.

Take, for example, the state of public finances during the recession that began in 2008. Many countries were mired in debates about which public expenditures to cut, and which – if any – to protect. Indeed, politicians of all varieties seemed to be falling over themselves to acquire the commander's mantle to inflict pain upon the profligate public sector wasters of our tax revenues. But this was to mistake the cause for the effect – the cause of the problem was the profligate investment bankers not the parsimonious public sector employees! Moreover, it is often the case that the same individual or group with authority will switch between the command, management, and leadership roles as they perceive – and constitute – the problem as critical, tame, or wicked, or even as a single problem that itself shifts across these boundaries. Indeed, this movement – often perceived as 'inconsistency' by the decision-maker's opponents – is crucial to success as the situation, or at least our perception of it, changes. That persuasive account of the problem partly rests in the decision-maker's access to – and preference for – particular forms of power, and herein lies the irony of 'leadership': it remains the most difficult of approaches, and one that many decision-makers will try to avoid at all costs.

The notion of 'power' suggests that we need to consider how different approaches to, and forms of, power fit with this typology of authority. Amongst the most useful for our purposes is Etzioni's typology of compliance, which distinguished between coercive, calculative, and normative compliance. Coercive or physical power was related to 'total' institutions, such as prisons or armies; calculative compliance was related to 'rational' institutions, such as companies; and normative compliance was related to institutions or organizations based on shared values, such as clubs and professional societies. This compliance typology fits well with the typology of problems: critical problems are often associated with coercive compliance; tame problems are associated with calculative compliance; and wicked problems are associated with normative compliance – you cannot force people to follow you in addressing a wicked problem because the nature of the problem demands that followers have to want to help.

This typology can be plotted along the relationship between two axes, as shown in Figure 2, with the vertical axis representing increasing uncertainty about the solution to the problem – in the behaviour of those in authority – and the horizontal axis

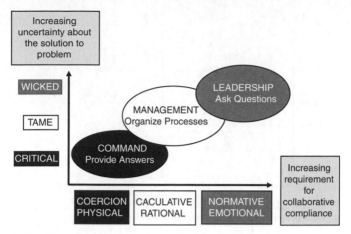

2. **Typology of problems, power, and authority**

representing the increasing need for collaboration in resolving the problem.

This might be regarded as obvious to many people – but if it is, why do we remain unable to effect such change? To answer that, I want to turn to cultural theory and explore some so-called 'elegant solutions'.

Culture and addiction to elegance

Mary Douglas argued that we could probably capture most cultures on the basis of two discrete criteria: grid and group. 'Grid' relates to the significance of roles and rules in a culture – some are very rigid, such as a government bureaucracy, but others are very loose or liberal, such as an informal club. 'Group' relates to the importance of the group in a culture – some cultures are wholly oriented around the group, such as a football team, while others are more individually oriented, such as a gathering of

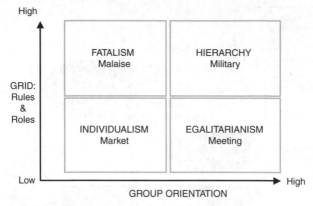

High

GRID:
Rules
&
Roles

Low

FATALISM Malaise	HIERARCHY Military
INDIVIDUALISM Market	EGALITARIANISM Meeting

GROUP ORIENTATION

High

3. **Four primary ways of organizing social life**

entrepreneurs. When these points are plotted on a two-by-two matrix, we derive Figure 3.

When a culture embodies both 'high grid' and 'high group', we tend to see rigid hierarchies, such as in the military, in which individuals are less relevant than the group. When the culture remains 'high group'-oriented but lacks the concern for rules and roles in 'low grid', we see egalitarian cultures, epitomized by those organizations in which the group meeting is sacred and the search for consensus critical. When the 'grid' remains low and is matched by an equal indifference to the 'group', we tend to see individualist cultures – the land of entrepreneurs, rational choice, and market-loving politicians for whom any notion of the collective or rules is perceived as an unnecessary inhibitor of efficiency and freedom. The final category is that of the fatalist, where the group dimension is missing and the isolated individuals believe themselves to be undermined by the power of rules and roles.

As so defined, such cultures tend to be self-supporting and philosophically consistent. In other words, hierarchists perceive the world through hierarchist lenses, such that problems are understood as manifestations of the absence of sufficient rules or the lack of enforcement of rules by the group or society. In contrast, egalitarians see the same problem as one connected to the weakness of the collective community – it is less about rules and more about the community generating greater solidarity to solve the problem. Individualists would have little faith in this; the problem is obviously (for them) to do with the individuals – individuals should be more responsible for their own situation. Fatalists, however, have given up, for the rules are against them and there is no group to help them out of their malaise.

Now the problem is that such internally consistent – or elegant – modes of understanding the world are fine for dealing with critical or tame problems because we know how to solve them and previous approaches have worked. Individualists can solve the problem of decreasing carbon emissions from cars – a tame problem open to a scientific solution; but they cannot solve global warming – a wicked problem. Egalitarians can help ex-offenders back into the community – a tame problem; but they cannot solve crime – a wicked problem. And hierarchists can improve rule enforcement for the fraudulent abuse of social services – a tame problem; but they cannot solve poverty – a wicked problem. Indeed, wicked problems don't offer themselves up to be solved by such elegant approaches precisely because these problems lie outside and across several different cultures and institutions. But because we are prisoners of our own cultural preferences, we become addicted to them and have great difficulty stepping outside our world to see something differently. As Proust put it: 'the real voyage of discovery consists not in seeking new landscapes but in having new eyes'.

Why elegant approaches don't solve wicked problems but clumsy solutions might

If single-mode (elegant) solutions can only ever address tame or critical problems, we need to consider how to adopt all three in what are called clumsy solutions. In fact, we need to eschew the elegance of the architect's approach to problems – start with a clean piece of paper and design the perfect building anew – and adopt the world of the *bricoleur*, the do-it-yourself craftworker. Or to adopt the rather more prosaic language of the philosopher Immanuel Kant, we need to begin by recognizing that, 'out of the crooked timber of humanity no straight thing was ever made'. Let us take global warming to illustrate this.

Figure 4 summarizes the issue. Hierarchists consider the problem to be a result of inadequate rules and their enforcement – a better Kyoto-style agreement is necessary. But egalitarians might argue that it isn't the rules that need altering and enforcing but our communal attitude to the planet that needs to change – we must develop more sustainable ways to live, not just obey the rules better. But for individualists, both alternatives misunderstand the problem – and therefore the solution is to carve out the freedoms that will encourage entrepreneurs to generate the technological innovations that will save us. For fatalists, of course, there is no

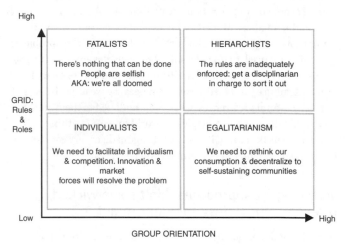

4. **Elegant (single-mode) solutions to global warming**

hope – we are all doomed. The problem here is that none of these elegant solutions actually generates sufficient diversity to address the complexity of the problem. Rules might facilitate safe driving, but they would probably not be effective in saving the planet. Nor can we simply abandon our centralized cities and all live in self-sufficient communities in the countryside. Similarly, although technological innovations will be critical and market pressures may help, we cannot rely on these to solve the problem. Indeed, global warming may not be solvable, in the sense that we can go back to the beginning and reclaim an unpolluted world, and because different interests are at stake in different approaches to the 'solution', the best we can hope for is a politically negotiated agreement to limit the damage as soon as possible. That calls for a non-linear, nay 'crooked', response, to stitch together an inelegant, or clumsy, solution combining all three modes of understanding, and making use of the fatalists' acquiescence to go along with the changing flow of public opinion and action. As shown in Figure 5, what we actually need is to use all three frameworks to make progress here, through the creation of a 'clumsy solution space'.

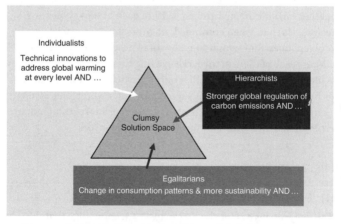

5. Clumsy solution for the wicked problem of global warming

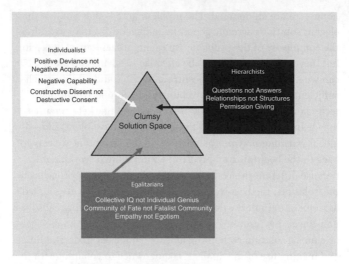

Individualists
Positive Deviance not Negative Acquiescence
Negative Capability
Constructive Dissent not Destructive Consent

Hierarchists
Questions not Answers
Relationships not Structures
Permission Giving

Clumsy Solution Space

Egalitarians
Collective IQ not Individual Genius
Community of Fate not Fatalist Community
Empathy not Egotism

6. **Clumsy approaches to wicked problems**

So what would a clumsy solution actually look like? Figure 6 implies that a critical component of a necessarily clumsy solution is to combine elements of all three cultural types: the individualist, the egalitarian, and the hierarchist. Within each of these types are techniques that, when combined, might just prise the wicked problem open far enough to make some progress with it. Let us address each of these in turn, recognizing that each wicked problem is likely to be different and that only a particular combination of techniques and issues might succeed. In other words, this is not a 'painting-by-numbers' approach to guarantee a resolution but an experimental art form that may – or may not – work.

Hierarchists

H1: Questions not answers

The first step here is for the hierarchist to acknowledge that the leader's role has to switch from providing the answers to asking the questions. The leader, then, should initiate a different narrative that prepares the collective for collective responsibility. Indeed, the reason that this sits within the hierarchists' camp is that only the hierarchical leader has the authority to reverse his or her contribution from one of answers to questions. Linked to this switch in approaches from expert to investigator is a related requirement that hierarchists are most suited for: relationships not structures.

H2: Relationships not structures

Traditionally, change models imply that if failure occurs despite the model, it must be because the leader has failed to pull the right levers in the right sequence. But this machine metaphor is precisely why leaders find change so difficult – because power is not something you can possess and thus there are no levers to pull. Power is a relationship, and change depends upon the relationships between leaders and followers: in effect, it is followers who make or break change strategies, not leaders alone, because organizations are systems not machines.

H3: Permission-giving

The traditional authority of the formal leader remains a significant inhibitor of followers' discretion: unless the boss has told you that open debate and disagreement about work issues are welcome – and then demonstrated that by not disciplining those engaged in constructive dissent – then there probably will not be much debate, and subordinates will allow their organizations to founder because they have not been given permission to save the boss. This is why hierarchists are critical to the clumsy methodology – because they have to authorize a change to the norm.

Individualists

I1: Positive deviance not negative acquiescence

Individualists are often those who deviate from the norm, and this behaviour can be critically important. For instance, in 1990, Jerry and Monique Sternin went to Vietnam for the charity Save the Children. Why, the Sternins wondered, were some children well nourished in the midst of general malnourishment? Mainstream Vietnamese culture generated a very conventional wisdom on malnutrition – it was the combined effect of poor sanitation, poor food distribution, poverty, and poor water. On the other hand, some children – and not the highest-status children – were well nourished because their mothers – the positive deviants – ignored the conventional culture that mothers should:

- avoid food considered as low class/common – such as field shrimps and crabs;
- not feed children who had diarrhoea;
- let children feed themselves, or feed them twice a day at the most.

Instead, these mothers:

- used low-class/common food – which was very nutritious;
- fed children who had diarrhoea – it's critical to recovery;
- actively fed children many times during the day (self-fed children drop food on the floor, so it's contaminated, and children's stomachs can take only a finite amount of food at any one time, so even feeding them twice a day is inadequate).

In short, the problems in organizations are often self-generated, but the solutions are often there too, it's just that usually we tend not to look for them.

I2: Negative capability

While hierarchists tend to be uncomfortable with ambiguity, individualists thrive on it. The poet Keats called 'negative capability' the ability to remain comfortable with uncertainty, and wicked problems are inherently uncertain and ambiguous, so the real skill is not in removing the uncertainty but in managing to remain effective despite it. In short, negative capability generates the time and space to reflect upon the issue and not to have to react to somebody else's agenda or to be decisive – but decisively wrong. Stein's comparison of decision-making in the Apollo 13 space mission and at Three Mile Island captures this issue well in situations in which experience is critical to providing help in stressful situations. Thus the 'cosmology episodes' that strike both Apollo 13 and Three Mile Island – when 'the world no longer seems a rational, orderly system' – provoke different responses from those responsible for decision-making. The 'cosmology episode' on Apollo 13 – an explosion – left the astronauts short of food, oxygen, power, water, and hope. But avoiding the natural temptation to jump to conclusions, the ground crew, through slow, careful analysis of the problems – and through the construction of a makeshift carbon dioxide scrubber (typical of the *bricoleur*'s approach) – enabled Apollo 13 to return safely. In contrast, in the 1979 Three Mile Island nuclear disaster, the 'cosmology episode' led to instant actions being taken which unwittingly made the situation worse. In effect, the decision-makers were decisive but wrong, and just to compound the situation, they then denied any evidence suggesting that the problem had not been resolved. So the ability to tolerate anxiety and to ensure that it does not become excessive (leading to panic) or denied (leading to inaction) generated different sense-making actions in these scenarios.

13: Constructive dissent not destructive consent

Finally, individualists are excellent at resisting the siren calls of both hierarchists and egalitarians to fall in line, either to the rules or the group. Since Milgram's and Zimbardo's infamous compliance experiments in the 1960s, we have known that most people, most of the time, comply with authority, even if that leads to the infliction of pain upon innocent others – providing the rationale is accepted by the followers, they are exempt from responsibility, and they only inflict pain ('engage in harm') incrementally. Put another way, the difficulty for our leader facing a wicked problem is not of securing consent but dissent. Consent is relatively easily acquired by an authoritarian, but it cannot address wicked problems because such consent is often destructive, and destructive consent is the bedfellow of irresponsible followership and a wholly inadequate frame for addressing wicked problems. What we actually need is constructive dissenters who are willing to tell their boss that his or her decision is wrong (as, for example, Field Marshal Alan Brooke frequently did with Winston Churchill during the Second World War). So what about egalitarians – why do we need them?

Egalitarians

E1: Collective intelligence not individual genius

Typically, we attribute both success and failure to individual leaders. In fact, the more significant the success or failure, the more likely we are to do this, even though we usually have little evidence for linking the event to the individual. Yet when we actually examine how success or failure occurs, it is more often than not a consequence of social rather than individual action. For example, Archie Norman, the British retail entrepreneur, rescued Asda from near bankruptcy in 1991 and sold it to Wal-Mart for £6.7bn in 1999. But underlying this phenomenal success was not the work of an isolated individual genius but a talented team, including, at board level: Justin King (subsequently CEO Sainsbury), Richard Baker (subsequently CEO Boots), Andy Hornby (subsequently CEO HBOS, then Boots), and Allan Leighton (subsequently Chair Royal Mail). In short, Asda's success was built on collective intelligence not individual genius. This approach is particularly important to wicked problems because they demand the collective responses typical of systems not individuals – it is the community that must take responsibility and not displace it upon the leader.

E2: Community of fate not a fatalist community

Anne Glover, a local community leader in Braunstone, Leicester, UK, is credited with turning her own fatalist community into a 'community of fate' when she mobilized her local neighbours to unite against a gang of youths engaging in antisocial behaviour and ruling their council estate through fear. Such fear had effectively demobilized the community, turning it into a disparate group of isolated individuals – a fatalist community – all complaining about the gang problem but feeling unable to do anything about it. When Glover persuaded a large group to go out – as a group – and confront the gang, the gang moved on and its members were eventually removed from the estate. There is more to this than simply being brave enough to do something and willing to take the risk that it will not be easy; it is about recognizing the importance of building social capital to nurture a collective identity which generates a community of fate.

E3: Empathy not egotism

Finally, the last egalitarian technique lies in the ability to step into another's shoes, to generate an empathy that facilitates understanding of the other and is a pre-requisite for addressing wicked problems, but how might we acquire it? Jones's answer is to become an anthropologist of your own organization, to walk a mile in the shoes of those whom you lead, to experience the life of those whom you want to engage in the collective effort, because if you cannot understand how they see the problem, how can you mobilize them? This is radically different from our usual methods for acquiring knowledge about how our organizations work, because we know that what people say in focus groups or in surveys does not represent how they normally see the world. Many CEOs and corporate leaders already work on their own shop-floor for a regular period of time – but many more do not, and then find themselves surprised when the bottom of the hierarchy doesn't respond in the way that the focus group or latest staff survey had predicted.

Conclusion

The complexity of many contemporary issues appears to justify this shift from tame problems and elegant solutions to the clumsy solutions more suited to addressing wicked problems. But in fact, many, indeed most, issues are tame not wicked and require people only to carry out their normal duties – without the help of bosses wielding long screwdrivers to micro-manage them. A real danger is that we become prisoners of our own cultural preferences – hierarchists become addicted to command, egalitarians become addicted to collaborative leadership, and individualists become addicted to managing all problems as if they were all tame. In effect, we become addicted to elegance, when we ought to be cultivating a clumsy approach if and when our own approaches prove inadequate to the task. This might explain why we find change so difficult – because, for example, when public sector organizations work collaboratively in partnerships to address wicked problems, like alcohol abuse or antisocial behaviour, the various partners fail (or refuse) to authorize each other to take the lead. Similarly, when nations try to address global problems, like global warming, the same egalitarian inhibition often stymies progress. One way of rethinking our approach to this is to recognize that hierarchists also have a part to play: collaborative leadership still requires someone or somebody to take a lead. As the State of California has discovered, when it requires a bare majority of those who bother to vote to increase public expenditure but a two-thirds majority of the legislature to increase tax revenues (or set a budget), sometimes you can have too much egalitarianism. But was it always thus? Did leaders lead in very different ways in past times? The next chapter addresses these questions.

Chapter 3
What was leadership?

Why bother with the beginning? Indeed, what counts as the beginning? Well we can start by suggesting that 'the beginning' for leadership scholars is the beginning of recorded history, not the beginning of *Homo sapiens*. As far as it is possible to tell, all organizations and societies of any significant size and longevity have had some form of leadership, often, but not always, embodied in one person – usually, but not always, a man. This does not necessarily mean that leadership has always been, and will always be, critical or essential, let alone masculine, but it does imply that we have always had leaders. How, then, can we establish whether leadership *is* crucial, or whether the forms and styles of leadership have changed across space and time?

To a very large extent, our knowledge of leadership in ancient times is crucially dependent upon the existence of written texts, and here lies the first lesson of leadership: history is written, generally speaking, by the winners. This goes for both successful military leaders and for successful political groups. In the former category, we might consider how we know so much about the victories of Alexander the Great or Julius Caesar, so little about Spartacus, and almost nothing about the hundreds of slave revolts that regularly shook slave societies throughout antiquity. The answer, of course, is that Alexander and Julius Caesar either wrote their own histories or had them professionally written at their behest, while Spartacus left no written accounts, and very few other slave leaders even get a mention in the accounts of their slave owners. Thus, a preliminary warning in reading any account of classical leadership – and indeed any account of contemporary leadership – is to be wary of the sources. Accounts are not neutral carriers of factual information; rather, they are partial accounts intended to achieve a particular purpose.

Whether that story ever gets written in the first place depends, to some extent, on whether the narrative contains something regarded as significant. That is to say, we tend to record only those events that are unusual or extraordinary to some degree. As a consequence, we do not have vast tracts on how to run a small farm in China 2,000 years ago, nor on leadership in an era of relative peace amongst the Celtic tribes of Gaul at the same time. But we do have records of the Celtic wars against the Romans at the time, and we do have some accounts of Chinese warlords in the same period. However, the texts relating to the wars between the Gauls and the Romans are Roman texts; first, because the Celts were largely a non-literate society in which oral cultures prevailed, and second, because, by and large, the Romans were victorious. Again, what tends to survive over long periods of time are material texts and artefacts rather than oral narratives, so our understanding of the leadership of non-literate societies is often reconstructed from the often pejorative accounts of others. From what we know of pre-literate ancient civilizations from the archaeological records, any periods of peaceful coexistence with neighbouring tribes led by humanitarian leaders are few and far between.

It seems clear, then, that war was a critical component in the early developments of the practice of leadership. From Sargon of Akkad (c. 2334–2279 BC) in what is now the Middle East, to Ramses II the Great of Egypt, and from the early Cretan civilizations from around 3000 BC to the Harrapan civilization in the Indus valley at the same time, and across to the Huang Ho walled settlements in China, we know that military leadership played a crucial role in the quest for survival and domination. Again, this is not to insist that leadership has its origins in war or that military leadership is the most important element in classical leadership – we simply do not know enough about these times to confirm or deny this. But it remains the case that some of the most important classical writings on leadership pertain either to the conduct of war, what the Prussian military theorist Carl von Clausewitz referred to as 'the continuation of policy by other means', or the conduct of politics itself. This is particularly so for the Classical and Renaissance periods that we shall consider first, before turning to the more modern literature.

Classical leadership studies

Outside Europe, Kautilya's *Arthashastra*, written around 321 BC for the Mauryan dynasty in what is now India, provided an array of practical tips for leaders to consider. But probably the first prescriptive text that achieved significant success in both its own time and space, ancient China, and *continues* to beguile business executives to this day is Sun Tzu's (?400–320 BC) *The Art of War*. In fact, it is not clear who the author of the aphorisms that comprise *The Art of War* really is, and it may be that many were written by Sun Tzu's disciples and students; indeed, the text reproduces this assumption in its conversational format, with several characters participating in the discussion under 'Master Sun's' facilitation. Nevertheless, the central message about leadership is clear: 'The responsibility for a martial host of a million men lies in one man. He is the trigger of its spirit' (*Manoeuvre* 20). Once this is established, *The Art of War* sets out to provide conversational sketches of the most crucial elements of strategy and tactics for military leaders.

Ironically, to Western minds, but appropriately for the minimalist essence of its Taoist origins, one of the most important lessons in *The Art of War* is that fighting is the last thing military leaders should engage in, for: 'those who win every battle are not really skilful – those who render others' armies helpless without fighting are the best of all' ('Planning a Siege'). Sun Tzu then insists that strategy is critical to success, for the art of war is the art of avoiding *unnecessary* conflict.

'The Golden Bridge' is a natural consequence of this philosophy: if you must fight, then avoid head-on conflicts if at all possible, since these are both expensive in resources and casualties and are far riskier than simply attacking the enemy's plans or supply lines. And if you must attack the enemy head-on – but you cannot be confident about a complete rout – then you should leave a 'golden bridge', an escape route for your enemy to retreat across, otherwise your enemy will be forced to fight to the finish, and again the consequences could be problematic.

A second and paradoxical piece of advice is to burn your own bridges: in other words, commit yourself or suffer the penalty. 'When a leader establishes a goal with the troops', suggests Sun Tzu, 'he is like one who climbs to a high place and then tosses away the ladder'. This is an inversion of the golden bridge rule, but that is for your enemies not your allies and followers, for if your colleagues feel threatened but see an easy escape route, they may well take it. If, however, there is no escape – what Sun Tzu refers to as 'Dead Ground' – then they will have to commit themselves to the fight for survival, and it is this commitment by followers to their leader that reflects the Taoist roots of Sun Tzu's work. As he puts it, in 'Nine Grounds': 'Put them in a spot where they have no place to go and they will die before fleeing.'

Sun Tzu is also adamant that military matters should be left to the military specialists and not to their political controllers. 'To say that a general must await commands of the sovereign in such circumstances is like informing a superior that you wish to put out a fire' ('Offensive Strategy'). Or, as is suggested in 'The Nine Variables', 'There are occasions when the commands of the sovereign need not be obeyed.... When you see the correct course act; do not wait for orders.'

At roughly the same time that Sun Tzu was teaching military leadership in China, Plato (427/428–347 BC) was warning the Greeks that the rise of political leadership rooted in democracy did not represent the flowering of Greek culture so much as a direct threat to Greek civilization. The electoral system for selecting leaders generated a circus rather than a forum for serious consideration, as far as Plato was concerned, for it encouraged potential leaders to pander to the basest instincts of the mob – 'the large and dangerous animal' – that pervades much of his writing in this sphere. The mob, suggests Plato in his *Republic*, would be willing to risk their society (represented as a ship) by electing whichever person promised them most. Thus, rather than sailing under the person who was best qualified to be the ship's captain (one of Plato's philosopher-kings), democracy ensures that the popular demagogue prevails – and, of necessity, leads the ship straight onto the rocks of catastrophe.

But how is the best person to lead recognized? For Plato, it is self-evident that we recognize the skills of people by considering their expertise: we would not ask a gardener to build us a boat any more than we would ask a farmer to run the economy. But, to Plato's intense frustration, where 'moral' knowledge is concerned, the mob assumes that everyone is an expert, and therefore no-one is. It was for precisely this reason that Plato was so firmly opposed to the Sophists and Isocrates who taught the skills of rhetoric, or public speaking, because this would simply encourage the domination of form over content. Above all, Plato feared that even those who intended to lead in a moral way for the benefit of the community would be corrupted by the system and, since leaders were vital to the health of the community, a corrupted leader would inevitably destroy 'his' own community. Aristotle (384–322 BC), one of Plato's students, agreed that Athens was indeed under attack from corrupt leaders but differed in his response to the problem. His book *Rhetorica* was written in part as an exposé of 'the tricks of public speaking', which Aristotle believed were already corrupting Athenian public life.

Renaissance leadership studies

Some 1,800 years after Aristotle, there emerged from that same area of the Mediterranean a book that came to dominate writing on leadership not just in its own time but in our time too. Not that Niccolò Machiavelli's *The Prince* was popular, on the contrary, it was the most *unpopular* prescriptive text of the 16th century. No doubt Machiavelli would have found this doubly ironic. First, because *The Prince* was written to regain some political credibility and popularity with his former employers; second, because Machiavelli wrote it as a descriptive, rather than a prescriptive, work. In other words, Machiavelli insisted that he wrote about the world of politics as it was, not as it should be in some mystical and unachievable utopia. It was the political realism that infused *The Prince* that led to its instant condemnation by the religious and political leaders of the day, but which also explains its popularity today. It was, according to Machiavelli, rooted not in theory but in historical fact, yet it was prohibited by the Catholic Church under its Index of Books.

The Prince was written in 1513–14 as Machiavelli's homeland fell apart under civil war and foreign invasion. Machiavelli sought to write a guidebook for all political leaders but, in particular, for the Medicis, his patrons and erstwhile leaders of Florence. *The Prince*, then, was not simply a book to ingratiate the favour of the Medicis, but a call to arms to defend Florence and – through Florentine domination – Italy, from the 'Barbarians', by whom he meant the Spanish and French invaders.

One of the principal role models that Machiavelli adopted for *The Prince* was Cesare Borgia, the illegitimate son of Rodrigo Borgia, who had become Pope Alexander VI in 1492. Cesare Borgia led the papal armies and threatened Florentine independence, but Machiavelli recognized a different category of leader in Cesare, for here was a man who murdered his own lieutenant (Remirro Orco), when he appeared to be unnecessarily cruel in his control over the Romagna. As Machiavelli recalled, '...one morning Remirro's body was found cut in two pieces on the piazza at Cesena, with a block of wood and a bloody knife besides it. The brutality of this spectacle kept the people of the Romagna at once appeased and stupified' (VII). Cesare subsequently invited those conspiring against him to dinner, only to have them all slaughtered as they ate. Machiavelli then used Cesare as a good example of realpolitik, for he believed Cesare had restored peace through the selective use of violence. The alternative, as professed in public by most leaders at the time, was to act nobly and morally, but for Machiavelli the consequence of acting morally in an immoral world was simply to allow the most immoral to dominate. 'The fact is', he suggests in *The Prince*, 'that a man who wants to act virtuously in every way necessarily comes to grief among so many who are not virtuous. Therefore if a prince wants to maintain his rule he must learn how not to be virtuous, and to make use of this or not according to need' (XV). Thus:

> Cesare Borgia was accounted cruel; nevertheless, this cruelty of his reformed the Romagna, brought it unity and restored order and obedience. On reflection it will be seen that there was more compassion in Cesare than in the Florentine people who, to escape being called cruel, allowed Pistoia to be devastated...
>
> (XVII)

In effect, Machiavelli was not suggesting that leaders should act immorally, but that to protect the interests of a community (a point more clearly covered in *The Discourse on Livy*) a prince has to do whatever is necessary – for the greater good. Thus the act should be contextualized and not analysed against some mythical moral world. The problem, of course, is defining 'the greater good'.

And, in answer to his rhetorical question 'whether it is better to be loved or feared, or the reverse', Machiavelli unequivocally sides with the fear factor.

> The answer is that one would like to be the one and the other; but because it is difficult to combine them, it is far better to be feared than loved if you cannot be both. One can make this generalization about men; they are ungrateful, fickle, liars and deceivers ... when you are in danger they turn against you. Any prince who has come to depend entirely on promises and has taken no other precautions ensures his own ruin. . . . The bond of love is one which men ... break when it is to their advantage to do so; but fear is strengthened by a dread of punishment which is always effective. The prince must nonetheless make himself feared in such a way that, if he is not loved, at least he escapes being hated.
>
> (XVII)

Modern leadership studies

Thomas Carlyle – for many, the first 'modern' writer on leadership – had spoken warmly at his inaugural address as Rector of Edinburgh University in 1866 of both Machiavelli and of Oliver Cromwell, whom Carlyle likened to just one of these princes who was absolutely necessary at the time of the English Civil War. In fact, we can trace the rise of leadership studies in the modern era – that is coincident with the rise of industrial societies – to the earlier 1840 lectures of Carlyle, whose fascination with the 'Great Men' of history effectively reduced the role of mere mortals to 'extras'. This model of individual heroism that he constructed personified a popular assumption about leadership in Victorian times: it was irredeemably masculine, heroic, individualist, and normative in orientation and nature. It was rooted in what you should do according to the cultural prescriptions of the day; indeed, not dissimilar to the same model that had littered the Classical and early modern periods.

That model seems to have prevailed throughout the latter half of the 19th century and was not really challenged until the first professional managerial group began displacing the original – and 'heroic' – owner-managers towards the end of the 19th century. Then, the argument runs, the context – and thus the 'requirement' – for leadership shifted from heroic individuals to rational systems and processes as the scale of industry and the level of backward integration began generating huge industries (especially in the USA) that needed significant numbers of administrators to retain organizational coherence. Many of the models for such organizational leadership were derived from the army, civil service, post office, and railways, and most constituted leadership as administrative positions within formal hierarchies. In turn, as the productive growth unleashed by these giants began to encourage significant market competition and eat into profit margins, attention quickly turned to cost-reduction strategies and to scientific management. F. W. Taylor, the founder of scientific management, concentrated on the control of knowledge by management at the expense of the workforce, and the deskilling of jobs in line with the expansion of the division of labour. In this case, leadership was configured as 'knowledge leadership', with the leaders as repositories of knowledge of production that generated power over production – in contrast to the control over production formerly wielded by craftworkers.

The economic depression of the 1920s coincided with the next major shift in leadership models and, for our purposes, it was a major shift back to the role of normative power and away from the rationality of scientific systems and processes that had dominated for the previous two decades. This 'return' to a previous normative model was derived initially from the Hawthorne experiments in the 1920s and 1930s at the General Electric (GE) plant near Chicago. There, Taylorist scientific experiments in the development of the optimum environmental working conditions had allegedly generated first perplexity and then a realization that work could not be measured objectively because the very act of measurement altered the experience and thus the behaviour of those being measured. This 'Hawthorne effect', as it was called, then spawned a whole series of related experiments that eventually persuaded first GE and then whole swathes of American management that workers were normatively not rationally motivated, and group-oriented not individually oriented in culture.

Arguably, these alternating models of leadership – first, the 'normative' model of Carlyle of the second half of the 19th century, followed by the 'rational/scientific' model of Taylor and Ford in the first two decades of the 20th century, in turn superseded by a return to the 'normative' model of the Hawthorne experiments that solidified into the 'human relations' approach of the 1930s and 1940s – reflect two broader phenomena: first, the economic cycles of the period; and second, the political models of the period. These economic cycles form the basis of Kondratiev's controversial theory of long economic waves; the political cycles are less controversial and more intriguing, for it seems unlikely that industry could have isolated itself from the global rise of the mass movements of communism and fascism in the late 1920s and 1930s, and more likely that the leadership models embodied in these were refracted in industry through a zeitgeist that made sense at the time. In other words, in an era when mass political movements driven by normative adherence to the collective will – but manifest in cult-like loyalty to the party leader – were so prominent, it seemed perfectly natural to assume that the best way to lead an industrial organization was to mirror this assumption: work should be normatively rather than rationally organized – by groups led by leaders who prototypically embodied the same apparent desires as those held by the masses.

By the time the Second World War was over, and the economic boom returned, the model that began to dominate in the West shifted once again from the normative cult of mass and heroes – that had reflected the power of communism and fascism – to one dominated by rational analysis of the situation – a scientific approach more conducive to the war-fighting capabilities of the pre-eminent victor, the USA, and one located within its individualist culture. Thus, we see the rise of the American self-actualization movement, manifest particularly in Maslow's 'hierarchy of needs', which argued that leaders need to sort out their followers' health and safety before the followers will focus on 'higher' needs; and in McGregor's displacement of 'Theory X' (humans are selfish, so lead by dominating them) with 'Theory Y' (humans are cooperative, so lead by encouraging them).

The movement away from norms and back towards the rational understanding of contexts followed the increasing criticisms of traits as well as the work of the University of Michigan and the Ohio State studies. These latter provided the framework for a radical development: contingency theory. Under the general umbrella provided by contingency theory, the theoretical fragility of relying upon a potentially endless list of traits and superhuman charismatics was – ostensibly – dealt a crippling blow. From then on, what really mattered was not having the most charismatic leader leading the most adoring mass of followers, but having a rational understanding of the situation and responding appropriately: an argument we covered in the previous chapter.

Since the early days of this contingency approach, we have 'progressed' by returning to the importance of leaders working with the (normative) 'strong cultures' beloved of Peters and Waterman, then on to the (rational) pedagogy of the re-engineering revolution of the 1990s, and finally on to the contemporary development of transformational and inspirational leadership theories silhouetted by the rise of terrorism, global warming, the 'credit crunch', and political and religious fundamentalism. Such transformations also invoked the New Public Management of the 1980s and 1990s, under which, for example, the British public sector was ostensibly transformed from lethargic and bureaucratic leviathan to agile service deliverer

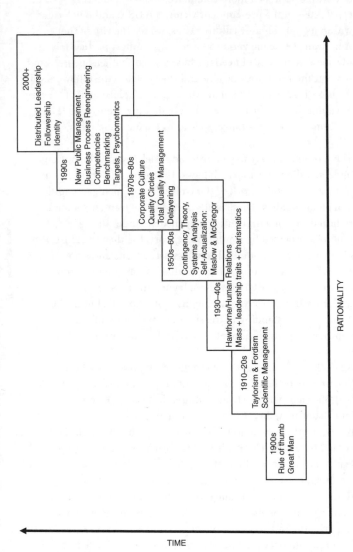

2000+
Distributed Leadership
Followership
Identity

1990s
New Public Management
Business Process Reengineering
Competencies
Benchmarking
Targets, Psychometrics

1970s–80s
Corporate Culture
Quality Circles
Total Quality Management
Delayering

1950s–60s
Contingency Theory,
Systems Analysis
Self-Actualization:
Maslow & McGregor

1930–40s
Hawthorne/Human Relations
Mass + leadership traits + charismatics

1910–20s
Taylorism & Fordism
Scientific Management

1900s
Rule of thumb
Great Man

RATIONALITY

TIME

7. **Increasingly rational leadership over time**

through the encroachment of the market and the discipline of
targets and performance-management systems.

Coupled with concerns about the importance of emotional
intelligence, identity leadership, and the development of inspiring
visions and missions, this seems to have ensured the return of
the original normative trait approaches: we seem to have gone
forward to the past. Thus, we were recently (back) in thrall to
inspirational individuals, endowed with whatever list of essential
competencies the contemporary leaders happen to have, that are
adjudged to be responsible for the catastrophic results.

Patterns of leadership

The argument for a dualist shift between forms of leadership is not
universally accepted. Indeed, there are many ways to understand
this pattern – if indeed there is a pattern. First, what we have is
simply an increasingly sophisticated and rational approach to
leadership across time represented by the incremental
enhancements manifest in Figure 7. Students of history will
recognize this as a Whig variant on progress across time.
Alternatively, there are two binary models that suggest a rather
different explanation for change: Figure 8 suggests that the pattern
is represented by a pendulum swinging between centralized and
decentralized models of leadership – usually premised on
assumptions about organizational learning and game-playing, so
that what was once efficient becomes inefficient as institutional
sclerosis sets in. Figure 9, on the other hand, retains the binary
model, but the causal mechanism relates to the structural binaries
that constitute language: night/day, black/white, dead/alive, and
so forth. Here it is the relationship between science and culture
which provides the natural linguistic barriers to change and, once
the efficiencies of one leadership style are expended, the pendulum
swings in the opposite linguistic direction until that mode is also
exhausted.

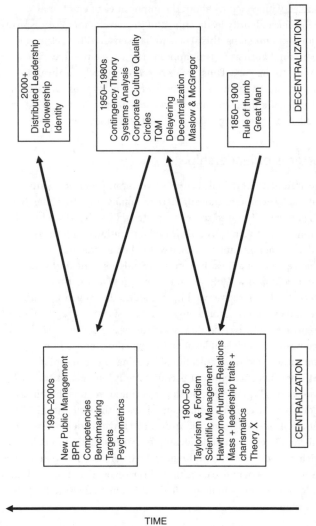

DECENTRALIZATION

2000+
Distributed Leadership
Followership
Identity

1950–1980s
Contingency Theory
Systems Analysis
Corporate Culture Quality
Circles
TQM
Delayering
Decentralization
Maslow & McGregor

1850–1900
Rule of thumb
Great Man

1990–2000s
New Public Management
BPR
Competencies
Benchmarking
Targets
Psychometrics

1900–50
Taylorism & Fordism
Scientific Management
Hawthorne/Human Relations
Mass + leadership traits + charismatics
Theory X

CENTRALIZATION

TIME

8. Binary model A: centralization–decentralization

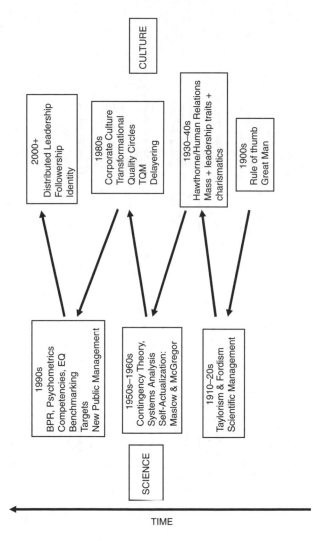

9. **Binary language model B: science versus culture**

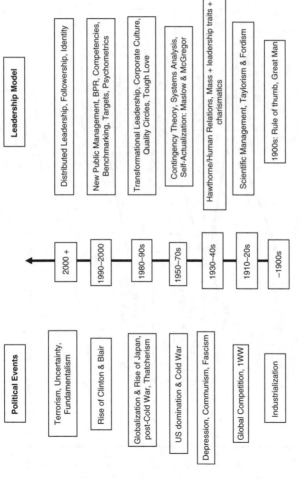

Leadership Model

Distributed Leadership, Followership, Identity

New Public Management, BPR, Competencies, Benchmarking, Targets, Psychometrics

Transformational Leadership, Corporate Culture, Quality Circles, Tough Love

Contingency Theory, Systems Analysis, Self-Actualization: Maslow & McGregor

Hawthorne/Human Relations, Mass + leadership traits + charismatics

Scientific Management, Taylorism & Fordism

1900s: Rule of thumb, Great Man

TIME

2000 +

1990–2000

1980–90s

1950–70s

1930–40s

1910–20s

–1900s

Political Events

Terrorism, Uncertainty, Fundamentalism

Rise of Clinton & Blair

Globalization & Rise of Japan, post-Cold War, Thatcherism

US domination & Cold War

Depression, Communism, Fascism

Global Competition, 1WW

Industrialization

10. Political zeitgeist

Fourth, a political model situates the changes not simply against the binary limits of language but also the political machinations of the wider context, in which what seems 'normal' only appears so when framed by the political ideologies of the day. This approach is represented in Figure 10. Thus Taylorism emerges as the norm, not simply because it is scientific and therefore rational, but because in an era when scientific breakthroughs were changing the world of work and when the eugenics movements started to dominate American culture, it seemed natural to assume that there was one best way to allocate, control, and lead labour. Similarly, when communism and fascism began to ensnare European politics, it seemed inevitable that the best way to lead was not through scientific management of the individual, but through the manipulation of the emotional mass by the charismatic leader. Once the Second World War was over, then the dominant power – the USA – reproduced its own scientific and individualist approach as the default leadership model, and only when the threat from Japan (re-)emerged in the 1980s was there a significant shift towards more cultural approaches to leadership. Once again, when these ran out of steam in the 1990s, the move was back towards the scientific end of the spectrum as New Public Management and target measurement took over, to be toppled only in the first decade of the 21st century as the spread of moral panics about global warming, financial catastrophes, political corruption, terrorism, and crime shift the debate back towards the cultural school of identity leadership and so on.

Finally, it might well be that there is no pattern at all, just an accumulation of historical detritus strewn around by academics and consultants hoping, at most, to make sense of a senseless shape or, at least, to make a living from constructing patterns to sell. It may be that the history of leadership is just one damned thing after another, but it could be worse: it could the same damn thing over and over again. Let us at least try and prevent the latter.

Chapter 4
Are leaders born or bred?

'Are leaders born or bred?' is probably the question that I am asked most frequently when teaching. My response is usually some variant of 'both': we really don't know enough about this to make any categorical statements one way or the other (though that doesn't stop people). What I want to do in this chapter is explore the question by generating a fourfold typology that expands the premise from 'nature or nurture' to include 'collective or individual'. This is not to sidestep the question but to be clear that any answer depends upon what kind of leadership we are talking about. We will start with the most traditional response: leadership is both individual and natural – Carlyle's approach – then consider a nurtured variant of this individualist approach, originally located in Athens. We then switch to consider collectivist approaches, beginning with the Athenians' 'natural' nemesis – the Spartans – and concluding with the Calchasian – the nurtured collectivists in a community of practice. A model of this typology is reproduced in Figure 11.

Shown in Figure 12 are two photos that relate to the question 'are leaders born or bred?' The first is of a school group in Georgia and the ringed figure is the young Stalin. The second is of a school group in Austria and the ringed figure is Hitler. The similar positioning of these two individuals in places of leadership – in the middle of the back row – is both alarming and coincidental. Stalin

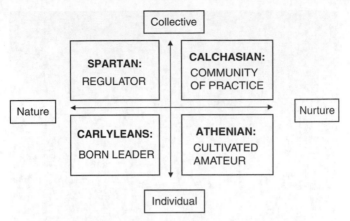

11. A typology of leadership development

is the boy who organizes the photographer, takes the fees, and pockets the profits – he appears to be a 'born' leader. Hitler plays no part in the organization of the photo; indeed, he is almost invisible at school – a waster going nowhere. In fact, Hitler's senior officer in the Bavarian Reserve Infantry Regiment, in which he served in the First World War, said of him at the time:

> Hitler did not cut a particularly impressive figure.... [but] he was an excellent soldier. A brave man, he was reliable, quiet and modest. But we could find no reason to promote him because he lacked the necessary qualities required to be a leader.... When I first knew him Hitler possessed no leadership qualities at all.
>
> (quoted in Lewis, 2003: 4)

Yet, within the space of a few years, Hitler turned into one of the most influential leaders of the 20th century. How did this happen? There are claims that Hitler – who was gassed by the British towards the end of the First World War – was taken out of the line and, along with many of his colleagues, proclaimed himself permanently

12. Stalin and Hitler. Stalin in his Tiflis seminary school (above) and Hitler in his Leonding school photo (below)

blinded. But while all the other soldiers insisted on being demobilized, Hitler demanded to return to the front. Now, since none of the soldiers were permanently blinded, the authorities knew most were literally trying to pull the wool over their eyes to escape a lost war, but they assumed that Hitler was suffering from some form of mental illness so he was sent to a psychiatrist. That psychiatrist, in turn, proclaimed that Hitler would only ever regain his sight if he was the 'chosen one' sent to save Germany. The story then unfolded with Hitler's returning sight and his gradual 'understanding' that destiny had saved him for something greater than being a corporal in the army. Whether this particular episode is true or not is not as important as considering the numbers of leaders who have achieved extraordinary things as a consequence of their belief in some form of destiny. Whether that destiny is one foretold by god (Jean d'Arc, Oliver Cromwell, Martin Luther King, Florence Nightingale) or by some force of history (Genghis Khan, Nelson, Stalin, General Patton, Winston Churchill) is less critical than its effect: it seems to generate a level of self-confidence that facilitates inordinate risk-taking, both of which are understood by followers as manifestations of great leadership. Of course, many of these 'predestined' leaders take risks and die in the process of their execution – but we don't get to hear about them. Instead, it is only the successful ones who survive, and these are the ones who bewitch us with their tales of destiny. In these cases, the question 'are leaders born or bred?' is actually redundant, because they may have been born 'ordinary' but have become transformed into 'extraordinary' by some kind of experience. But how important are these kinds of leaders?

The Carlylean: the born leader

Thomas Carlyle (1795–1881) was adamant that 'true' leaders – heroes – were born not made. The masses – who were 'full of beer and nonsense' – were incapable of generating their own leaders and the new capitalist bosses – 'the millocracy' – were only interested in the accumulation of material wealth. For Carlyle, great leaders did not emerge through privileged enculturation or education but through individual raw – that is, 'natural' – talent combined with a Nietzschean 'will to power'. Carlyle's heroes were 'born to lead' but not 'born into greatness'; hence his list included Mohammed, Luther, Frederick (who *became*) the Great, Cromwell, and Napoleon – all (like himself) born with little except the 'natural will' and ability to lead. For, as Carlyle insisted:

> Universal History, the history of what man has accomplished in this world, is at bottom, the History of the Great Men, these great ones; the modellers, patterns, and in a wide sense creators, of whatsoever the general mass of men contrived to do or to attain; all things that we see standing accomplished in the world are properly the outer material result, the practical realization and embodiment, of Thoughts that dwelt in the Great Men sent into the world: the soul of the whole world's history, it may justly be considered, were the history of these.
>
> (Carlyle, 2007: 1)

Carlyle would probably have been sympathetic to contemporary evolutionary perspectives on leadership – a response mechanism to the problem of coordination in an era when survival required collective action for gathering food and protecting the group. The current activities of hunter-gather societies are probably the closest we can get to early models of human leadership during the Pleistocene era (roughly from 1.8 million ago to 10,000 years ago, the end of the last ice age) where semi-nomadic, kin-related groups of 50–150 *Homo sapiens* operated, probably spreading from their origins in Africa about 200,000 years ago. The development of settled agriculture after the end of the last ice age generated significant reserves and resources that may have generated a propensity to abandon both hunter-gatherer cultures and the egalitarian and participative leadership models that are associated with their contemporary variants. In short, the production of surpluses may have triggered the move to more static communities led by warlords whose ability to protect/exploit their communities – and destroy rivals – may have been what Hobbes had in mind when he talked about the war of all against all when life was 'nasty, brutish, and short'.

For evolutionary biologists, the selection of leaders under conditions of constant war would have focused upon a relatively small number of 'alpha-males' – Carlyle's 'heroes'. The subsequent forms of natural selection eliminate all but the fittest, or rather all but the most appropriate for leadership positions, but this also means that contemporary organizational forms are deemed to be 'inappropriate' for our (hardly) evolved forms of leadership. In effect, in this approach the requirements of leadership are hard-wired into humans and remain relatively stable across space and time.

Actually establishing what is or isn't hard-wired is extraordinarily difficult to do. First, it's quite difficult to assess people before they become affected by their upbringing – evaluating babies for their leadership skills is not easy. Moreover, some behaviours seem illogical: why, for instance, would you voluntarily subordinate yourself to a leader if the consequences for reproduction advantage the leader more than the follower?

Often, this approach relates the apparent universality and timelessness of human leadership to our animal nature because leadership in animals appears unchanging and tends to be amongst the most hierarchical and brutal. Leadership amongst lions, for example, is primarily undertaken by lionesses in terms of hunts and tending the young but the alpha-male dominates others in terms of eating and mating privileges. But not all animals have the same leadership patterns: in spotted hyenas, for instance, the gender roles are reversed – females are larger than the males, and it is the former who control the mating process and lead the group; males do most of the hunting, but females dominate the males and have priority access to kills made by the males. Some evolutionary approaches imply that the matriarchal domination of spotted hyena groups develop because the males play no role in bringing up the young; strange how no-one told the cheetahs this leadership strategy. Wolf packs are slightly different: family units of between two and twelve individuals are led by the alpha-pair which alone breeds. A strict hierarchy exists within wolf packs in which the alpha-male leads hunts and territorial defence while the alpha-female leads the pups.

But if human leadership is a mirror of the animal world, then we should most closely resemble the world of chimpanzees, our closest genetic cousins. Yet De Waal's account of chimpanzees suggests that leadership is not determined by size or necessarily by hard-wiring but by coalition-building between dominant males supported by senior females. Moreover, Boehm suggests that analysis of contemporary hunter-gathers suggests that leaders are always and everywhere resisted by 'reverse dominance hierarchies' – by coalitions who unite temporarily to resist tyrants. In effect, the legitimation of leaders depends upon the followers, not the leaders.

If we really are the 'victims' of our genes, then we might also want to question the notion of free choice or agency. Volition is the exercise of free will or conscious choice, as opposed to determinism, hence, if human action is determined by biological genes, then the intentional element of leadership is removed and we may have a problem in determining individual responsibility. In effect, we may have no responsibility and therefore no leadership. In fact, taking this approach to its logical conclusion in the case of biologically inherited characteristics would be to suggest that those leaders with 'criminal genes' are not responsible for their leadership of criminal gangs, even if the results are significant in terms of people killed or money stolen and so on. And if we insist that action is determined by biological requirements over which individuals have no volitional control, then we might even consider looking for the leadership gene that is *making* them act. The ancient Athenians would have had none of that; for them, leadership was something to cultivate not something to emerge naturally.

The Athenian: the cultivated amateur

The 'Athenian' refers to the model of leadership learning embodied by those citizens of Ancient Athens (male only) who acquired leadership position by dint of their relatively high social birth combined with a liberal education in the arts, suitably supported by 'character-building' physical education. The initial schooling period was from eight to fourteen years old, and richer boys then progressed until eighteen, when a two-year military service was the norm. The intention was to nurture (male) children, who through engagement in reflective learning, often in private, would provide the next generation of Athenian citizens with sophisticated and responsible leaders. These leaders regarded themselves as 'cultivated amateurs' – they were not the products of a sausage-factory educational system that poured forth professional soldiers like their arch-rivals the Spartans – but instead the most civilized product of the most civilized society. That the presence of slaves and the subordination of women might strike the contemporary reader as anything but civilized is another matter.

The consequence of this kind of 'cultivated' approach to leadership training in the British Army through the 19th century was an upper-class officer corps devoted to loyalty, hard work, and practicality – but little or no capacity for imagination and little interest in or support for science and technology. Thus its difficulties in the early part of the First World War, and the 1930s in particular, and the decline of Britain's technological lead in general. And where business and stalemated war required entrepreneurial and imaginative thought, instead it generated 'guardianship', a code of ethics that favoured responsibility and romantic idealism over innovative structures, procedures, and strategies. The result was an indifference to military theory or strategy and reliance upon the individual initiative of combat officers together with good British 'common sense'.

Leadership, then, was not something that subordinates might engage in – as the German Army had long been developing – but it was essentially rooted in an exchange mechanism: paternalism was exchanged for loyalty, dignity for deference. In effect, the leaders were obliged to treat their soldiers as they would their own children, and the soldiers would be obligated to obey their officers as *in loco parentis* in return. As one subaltern from the 1/King's suggested in 1914: 'How like children the men are. They will do nothing without us ... You will see from this some reason for the percentage of casualties among officers.' Hence privileges acquired by the officer corps were not necessarily resented by the soldiers – as long as the privileges did not undermine the social obligations of the officers to look after their men, and that often implied very small things, such as remembering a soldier's birthday, enquiring about his home life, and making sure the soldiers were all fed as well as possible.

The 'Spartan': the regulator

While the Carlylean and Athenian models are both essentially individualist leadership models, the former being natural and the latter being encultured, the Spartan is ruthlessly – if not obsessively – collectivist and overtly naturalist: leadership abilities were something that many Spartans were born with, but they had to be corralled to the benefit of the community, and they had to be enhanced in a collective framework. Moreover, leadership would only work effectively when the followers were trained into obedience through the same leadership system, regulated to follow the regulator. That regulation began at birth when a committee of elders assessed each infant, leaving those defined as 'weak' to survive or die on the slopes of Mount Taygetos overnight.

The Spartans placed all their male children from seven to eighteen years of age into the Agoge (*agôgé*) (literally, 'raising', as pertaining to animals), an institution that combined education, socialization, and training to turn boys into warriors. The content of Spartan education involved little reflective learning and the construction of loyalty to the state remained foremost. The primary aim of education for boys was the creation of a loyal, dedicated army, and at the age of thirteen they were commanded by one of the *irens* – twenty-year-old junior leaders whose experience in command was designed to instil Spartan leadership qualities amongst a large number of warriors. The younger boys were also required to go through the *Krypteia*, or 'period of hiding', when they lived alone or in small self-led groups living off the countryside and killing helots (Spartan slaves) who were regarded as particularly strong or likely to harbour leadership ambitions themselves. At the age of eighteen, a select group was appointed to the elite Royal Guard and thence to formal military leadership positions, though military training continued until the age of thirty. But even royalty in Sparta had a collective, rather than an individual, orientation: the five annual elected ephors – overseers – swore to support the dual kings but only if the kings maintained the rule of law. Thus, if one of the Spartan kings insisted on leading the army into battle, as he was permitted to do, two of the five ephors always accompanied him and reported back on his conduct.

The clearest connection to a more recent Spartan approach to selecting and collectivizing for leadership was probably the organizations making up the Hitler Youth movement. In the Adolf Hitler Schools, in particular, German boys were groomed for leadership on the battlefield and in the homeland. While one-third of Germans born between 1921 and 1925 died in the war, 50% of those attending the Adolf Hitler Schools died in the war. By 1935, 50% of all Germans aged between ten and eighteen were in the Hitler Youth, and 90% of all those born in 1926 were recruited. In fact, membership remained voluntary until 1939, but few resisted. Organized on military lines with groups of 150 comprising a company (*Fähnlein*) down to the ten-boy *Kameradschaft* (*Jungmädelschaft* for girls). 'Leadership of youth by youth' was Hitler's slogan, and nothing was left to chance: 12,727 Hitler Youth (*Hitlerjunge*) (aged fourteen to eighteen years) leaders, and 24,660 *Jungvolk* (aged ten to fourteen years) (*Jungmädel* for girls) leaders were put through 287 leadership training courses in 1934 alone. Once through the course of physical and military training and ideological conditioning, these young leaders were provided with manuals for their own followers, complete with introductions, songs, and texts for each lesson. No discussion or dissension was permitted, but the most important experience seems to have been the weekend and summer camps where the community-building developed in earnest, usually by ensuring that everyone from the age of twelve took turns to lead his *Kameradschaft* or her *Jungmädelschaft*. 'That way', wrote a member of staff at a boy's school, 'he learns to give orders and gains the subconscious strength of self-confidence which is necessary in order to command obedience.' After successful completion through the *Jungvolk* and *Hitlerjunge*, the chosen few went on to one of the *Ordensburg* (SS Colleges), where Sparta remained an ideal. 'What we trainers of young leaders want to see', said one trainer in 1937, 'is a modern form of government modelled on the ancient Greek city-state. The best 5 to 10 per cent of the population are selected to rule, and the rest have to work and obey.' These leaders in waiting then spent one year in the SS College at Vogelsang, learning 'racial philosophy', a further year at Crössinsee, 'character-building', and a final year in Sonthofen on administrative and military duties. It was at the 1935 passing-out parade that Robert Ley, the Nazi Party head of organization, commented:

> We want to know whether these men carry in themselves the will to lead, to be masters, in a word: to rule. The NSDAP [Nazi Party] and its leaders must want to rule ... we take delight in ruling, not in order to be a despot or to revel in a sadistic tyranny, but because it is our unshakeable belief that in all situations only one person can lead

and only one person can take responsibility. Power rests with this one person.

(quoted in Knopp, 2002)

For the Nazis, the ultimate 'one person', of course, was Hitler, and as the war progressed Hitler distanced himself from the collectivist essence of Nazism and from the pre-war German military philosophy (Mission Command) that supported subordinate initiative and feedback between leader and followers, and this played an important role in his nemesis. For instance, it is clear that from 1939 to 1941, the invasion of Poland, Western Europe, and the USSR, that Hitler engaged in conversations with his generals and listened to them – even if he did not always take their advice. And only on one occasion did Hitler personally intervene in the invasion of Poland – to be overruled by Von Rundstedt. However, once the invasion of the Soviet Union faltered in the winter of 1941, Hitler began 'micro-managing' the armed forces and stopped listening to his generals. Thus, as the war progressed, Hitler's conversations became increasingly one-sided and the information he received stopped coming from constructive dissenters and instead came from destructive consenters. That is to say, as the independent thinkers were removed from his circle of advisers, so the quality of the advice sank to the point where the only advice he received was that they thought he wanted to hear rather than that which he needed to hear.

In contrast, Winston Churchill, who began the Second World War in the admiralty and removed a certain Captain Talbot because he had the temerity to disagree with Churchill about the anti-U-boat strategy, began as prime minister by recruiting many of the individuals he knew to be the most independent and free-thinking. Hence, he asked Ernest Bevin, one of the leaders of the General Strike in 1926 that Churchill had sought to crush, to join the war cabinet as Minister of Labour and National Service. Indeed, he even worked with Chamberlain and Halifax, two of his bitterest political enemies. Similarly, in the military sphere, Churchill retained Alan Brooke despite their famous disagreements and furious disputes, because Churchill recognized that only such people had the fortitude – and stubborn independence – to give him the honest advice that he needed. This alternative way of learning to lead is a critical element of the fourth model of learning: the Calchasian.

The Calchasian: community of practice

The fourth leadership learning form – the Calchasian – combines a collective orientation with a nurture philosophy. In effect, it suggests that leaders are neither omniscient nor omnipotent, and therefore leadership has to be distributed through the organization; furthermore, such a deep or distributed approach can be encultured, it can be socially supported and we need not simply rely on 'nature' to take its course in the leadership stakes. This kind of approach also assumes that engagement in social practice is the fundamental process by which we learn, thus learning is a collective or social activity not an individual activity. Indeed, as Wenger has suggested, learning actually occurs through a 'community of practice' in which engagement in a social practice constitutes a social community and thus an identity which can then be led.

> Since the beginning of history, human beings have formed communities that accumulate collective learning into social practices – communities of practice. Tribes are an early example. More recent instances include the guilds of the Middle Ages that took on the stewardship of a trade, and scientific communities that collectively define what counts as valid knowledge in a specific area of investigation. Less obvious cases could be a local gardening club, nurses in a ward, a street gang, or a group of software engineers meeting regularly in the cafeteria to share tips.

(Wenger, quoted in Grint, 2005: 115–16)

But a community of practice does not arise simply from physical proximity, and unless there is 'mutual engagement' of participants, that 'community' will not develop a 'community of practice'. Moreover, a community of practice is not a utopian ideal where mutuality and love prevail, but one defined by shared practice and collective repertoires rather than harmonious relationships.

I want to suggest, further, and in an inversion of our common assumptions about this relationship, that it is followers who teach leadership to leaders. In effect, it is not just experience that counts, but reflective experience. This inverse learning is mirrored in the way most parents learn to be parents: their children teach them. Or as Gerard Manley Hopkins suggests, 'The child is father to the man'. Hopkins seems to be implying that the male child will literally grow into the man, in the same way that an acorn grows into an oak tree. But I want to suggest a different interpretation here: that the child teaches his or her progenitors to be parents.

Although many books exist on parenting, a large proportion of learning to be a parent can only come from the experience of 'parenting'. After all, you cannot know whether somebody else's method works until you try it on your own child. In theory, parents teach their children how to act as children, but of course the latter have a way of ignoring much of this worthy advice. If this was not the case, then no parent would ever have misbehaving children, no child would have a tantrum on the supermarket floor, no teenager would experiment with alcohol or drugs, and none would come home late or leave their room looking like a burglar has just ransacked the place. Since this does occur regularly, the superior resources of parents (physique, language, legal support, moral claims, source of pocket money, threats of grounding, and so on) have only limited effect. The critical issue, then, is that parents have to learn how to be parents by listening and responding to their children. In effect, we are taught to be parents by our children: if they don't feel comfortable with the way we are holding them as infants, they cry and we adjust our hold; if they are hungry, they cry and we feed them; if they are tired, they cry and we rock them to sleep. And when – not if – we get it wrong (or they think we get it wrong), they tell us, by crying or struggling or sulking or whatever. Of course, we then have to decide what to do, whether to 'teach them' some self-control or whatever, but whether that works or not is not solely in our control, and we often have to negotiate our way through this continually changing relationship. Indeed, although experience might make parenting easier – the more children you have, the easier it might become – this need not be the case, perhaps because each child–parent relationship is different, and/or because each new child alters the pattern of prior familial relationships, and/or because some people have problems learning.

What might be crucial here is the extent to which parents receive feedback from their children. It may also be that parents learn most from relationships with their children that are not hugely asymmetric. In other words, when children are dominated by their parents – or vice versa – neither side in the relationship necessarily learns much or matures. Indeed, it may be that one of the reasons why so many parents do seem to make a relatively good job of a very difficult task is because children are often more open and honest in their feedback than adult followers or subordinates: if parents are not doing something 'properly' – as defined by the children not by the parents – the parents will soon hear about it. This is evident both with toddlers, who can be excruciatingly honest in their conversations, and when we meet the children of people we perceive as formidable leaders: so often, their children seem capable of saying things to them that we poor followers dare not even think about saying to them. If we map this learning model onto leadership, the implication is that, while leaders think they are teaching followers to follow, in fact it is the followers who do most of the teaching and the leaders who do most of the learning. Here, then, we might reconstruct Gerard Manley Hopkins: 'The follower is teacher to the leader.'

Inevitably, some leaders fail to learn and some followers fail to teach, but it may well be that one of the secrets of leadership is not a list of innate skills and competencies, or how much charisma you have, or whether you have a vision or a strategy for achieving that vision, but whether you have a capacity to learn from your followers. And that learning approach is inevitably embedded in a relational model of leadership. I also want to suggest that the asymmetrical issue is critical to successful leadership. That is to say, where the relationship between leaders and followers is asymmetrical in either direction – weak/irresponsible leaders or weak/irresponsible followers – then success for the organization is likely to be short-lived because feedback and learning is minimized. In effect, learning is not so much an individual and cognitive event but a collective and cultural process.

As I intimated above, this problem of learning to lead from one's subordinates is not a novel idea and has, in fact, been evident in leadership since the Classical era. In Greek mythology, for instance, Calchas, the son of Thestor (a priest of Apollo) is a soothsayer to Agamemnon, King of Mycenae, in the Trojan War. Agamemnon, concerned to ensure success, approaches Calchas – a Trojan. Calchas then visits the Oracle at Adelphi and declares that victory for the Greeks can only be achieved at significant cost to Agamemnon: the sacrifice of his daughter Iphigenia, the task will take ten years, and no victory will ensue unless Achilles fights for the Greeks. Agamemnon, therefore, has to take on trust the words of a Trojan – a former enemy – because he cannot trust the information of his 'natural' allies, the Greeks.

This 'Calchasian' approach thus transcends one of the most critical weaknesses of leadership learning: the displacement of constructive dissent with destructive consent. By this, I mean that since no individual leader has the knowledge or power to lead effectively, leadership must be a collective affair. However, as leaders progress through organizational hierarchies, they tend to surround themselves with sycophants – the veritable 'yes-people'

THE ROAD TO WISDOM

The road to wisdom? – Well, it's plain
and simple to express:
Err
and err
and err again
but less
and less
and less.

13. The road to wisdom

who provide flattering feedback rather than honest feedback. In contrast, long-term organizational success requires constructive dissenters – individuals able and willing to provide formal leaders with potentially unpleasant but necessary feedback for leaders to learn how to lead. Agamemnon's problem is that only a non-Greek can provide this, and that provides a manifestation of the central problem for learning to lead: it requires those who are willing to stay out of the limelight, avoiding the individual heroic model of leadership beloved of Carlyle and the like, but simultaneously do a job that is in many ways 'heroic' by providing formal leaders with contrary advice, by refusing to be cowed by the authority of formal leaders, and by putting the needs of the community or organization before their own – an approach much closer to the leadership model employed by some American Indians.

So the issue is not 'How should an organization find a leader who does not make mistakes', but what kind of organization generates a supporting framework that prevents leaders making catastrophic mistakes and ensures that the organization learns from the mistakes that we all make. Not 'Who should lead us?', but 'What kind of organization do we want to build?' and 'How can we build it?' The assumption that failure is a critical component of learning also implies that we should develop leaders by putting them in difficult situations where risks are necessary, errors possible, and learning essential. Or, as the saying goes: 'Good judgment comes from experience and experience comes from bad judgment' (attributed to various people, including Mark Twain and Frederick P. Brooks). So do we have to design more opportunities for failure into learning to lead? Perhaps Piet Hein captures this approach best with his marvellous poem and cartoon, shown in Figure 13.

Chapter 5
Who are the leaders?

THWαMPs

According to Gladwell, Warren Harding, the 29th President of the USA, is also widely regarded as the worst President in US history. Three years of his administration achieved little, and Senator William G. McAdoo said that a typical Harding speech was 'an army of pompous phrases moving over the landscape in search of an idea'. After Harding left office, it became clear that scandal and corruption were never far away – yet during his tenure he remained popular. Gladwell suggests this relates to a common temptation to relate first impressions of physique and personality to potential success. Since Harding was the archetypal tall and handsome (T&H) leader, and a confident (if vacuous) speaker, people naturally attributed great things to him in the same way that we attribute organizational success to individual leaders, often with little or no evidence that the correlation is actually a causation. In fact, there are strong correlations between body and attributive assumptions. For example, Gladwell's own analysis of Fortune 500 companies found that most of the CEOs were white males with an average height of just under six feet. In fact, almost 60% were six foot or taller, compared to a mere 15% of the rest of American adult males. So can we start by assuming that most Western leaders seem to be tall handsome white males, or THWMs?

Not necessarily. Despite the common assumption that height makes a significant difference to how leaders are perceived (the taller, the better), there have been lots of small leaders. For example, Ben Gurion and Deng Xiaoping were all 5 foot (1.52 metres); Yasser Arafat, Mahatma Gandhi, Kim Jong-il, King Hussein, Nikita Khruschev, and Dmitry Medvedev are or were all 5 foot 3 inches (1.6 metres); and Queen Elizabeth II, Franco, Haile Selassie, Silvio Berlusconi, Emperor Hirohito, Nicholas Sarkozy, Stalin, T. E. Lawrence, and Horatio Nelson are or were all under 5 foot 6 inches (1.66 metres). On the other hand, American research has consistently shown that taller people earn more than smaller people – in 2007, each extra inch of height was correlated with an extra 1% increase in income, and people with lighter skin colour earn more than those with darker skin colour.

Despite this, there are, and always have been, significant female leaders who have broken the male mould. There are, for instance, at the time of writing, 23 female heads of state from the 192 countries affiliated to the United Nations, and there were queens ruling Egypt in 3,000 BC. But these are often exceptions that prove the rule of male dominance across space and time.

So what kinds of characters do leaders seem to be now? Kaplan's analysis suggests an even more stereotyped model – CEOs are not just THWM but also archetypal alpha-males: aggressive, efficient, persistent, privileged, and uncompromising. So we can change our acronym now to tall handsome white alpha-males (of) privilege, or THWαMPs (which is easier to say than THWMs). Yet Kaplan's data are derived from CEOs of private equity firms ... the very arena that seems to be mired in financial disaster as I write. Perhaps this personality type explains why, according to Andrew Clark, five days after the world's largest insurance company, AIG, accepted an $85 billion emergency loan from the US government to stave off bankruptcy (17 September 2008), the company spent $440,000 on a week-long corporate retreat at one of California's top beachside resorts. Or, as Henry Waxman, chair of the US

Congressional Committee on Oversight and Government Reform, said to Richard Fuld, then CEO of Lehman Brothers, on 8 October 2008: 'Your company is bankrupt and our economy is in a state of crisis. Yet you get to keep $480m. I have a very basic question: Is that fair?' The following day, AIG was granted access to a further $37.8 billion from the US state; it must have been a great party. In fact, the party must still be in full swing: in 1999, the average ratio of CEO to employee pay in the UK rose from 47 to 128, with Bart Becht, CEO of Reckitt Benckiser, topping the show at 1,374 (Becht received £37 million in 2008, whilst the average employee salary of the Slough-based multinational was £26,700 – the UK's national average). Not that Becht needed to fear isolation: the average pay of the top 25 FTSE 100 directors in 2007/8 was over £10 million (as quoted in *The Guardian*).

Now the real issue here is not about fairness, if the implication is that treating followers as fellow humans rather than corporate resources is the way to lead successfully. That patently is not the case. There are lots of examples of success being driven through monstrous behaviour, by extraordinary cruelty, by slavery, and by many other 'unfair' leaders. Perhaps the point is twofold. First, fairness is only an appropriate criterion for judging leaders in contexts that are culturally associated with fairness. In crises, for example in war, survival is probably more important to most followers than fairness. But when the financial crisis struck the global markets in October 2008, the prior assumption about the importance of corporate success over fairness was reversed, and one of the reasons for the delay in passing the rescue package through the US Congress was because it was perceived to be unfair – to favour the bankers who had allegedly caused the problem at the expense of the tax-payers who were expected to rescue the bankers from their own mistakes. Second, returning to Chapter 2, we might suggest that the kind of leadership that works depends on (1) what the situation appears to require, and (2) how persuasive those same leaders can be in framing and reframing the situation so that it seems to call for the actions they themselves propose.

In many countries, fairness is often linked to diversity, yet in most of these same countries the level of diversity at the top is often marked by – diversity. For example, a poll by the *Observer* newspaper in October 2008 listed the top 100 most powerful black people in the UK, and the selection panel appears to have avoided the stereotypical listing procedures that would have filled the list with black pop stars and sports personalities. Instead, the selection was based on their 'influence', defined as: 'The ability to alter events and change lives.' Top of the men's list was Dr Mo Ibrahim, the entrepreneur who did more than anyone else to bring the mobile phone to Africa. While the women's list was headed by Baroness Scotland, who at school was told by a careers' adviser that being a supervisor at Sainsbury's was about her limit. She was the first black woman in Britain to become a Queen's Council (QC), and in 2007 became the first female Attorney General. As Trevor Phillips, Chairman of the Commission for Equality and Human Rights, and fifth on the men's list noted:

> It's important to show that there are people from minority communities who are playing a role in public life, ready to shoulder some of the burdens of the whole community, not just the narrow minority interest... There are two stereotypes: angry black men and suffering black women, and actually most of us are neither of those things. If people can stop thinking of black people they meet as fitting one of those two stereotypes, they might look past the front page, which is their colour, and look at the individual rather than think of them as a category. This kind of exercise helps to do that and will make a huge difference to a lot of people's lives.

In the USA, with Barack Obama currently in the White House, people of colour in 2008 comprised about one-third, or 34%, of the population. But as a proportion of the top elected government officials, such as Members of Congress, only 15% are African

American, Latino, Asian American, or American Indian, and only 24% are women. Things are little different in non-profit organizations, 84% of which are led by whites. Moreover, 42% of non-profit organizations serve only white communities. Traditionally, we have been led to believe that the problem is actually one best understood historically – of course, Western leaders used to be white men, but this is changing, albeit slowly, and soon we will see the emergence of greater diversity amongst out executive elite. Yet this is not at all self-evident.

Research undertaken by the Co-operative Asset Management in 2009 revealed that only 3% of the FTSE 350 companies had a woman as CEO (only four, or 1.3%, have female chairs), and 130 do not have any women at board level. Indeed, only 9% of board seats are taken by women – but it cannot be for want of an equal opportunities policy because 94% of the companies had them. In 2008, women occupied just under 10% of the board seats available on the top 300 European companies – but most of the limited growth that has occurred over the last few years can be explained not by the steady policies of diversity but, for example, by the legislative demands (from 2003) of Norwegian companies who are now required by law to have at least one woman on the board of all of its companies. In fact, Norway now has a 40% minimum target for all publicly listed companies. While the Scandinavian countries lead the gender equality movement, the rest of Europe lags some way behind.

In the USA, women represent half of those people in professional and managerial positions, but there is a familiar pattern beyond the general statement of equality: women tend to be better represented within charities and the public sector, but the higher up the ladder one looks, the fewer women are visible. For example, only 15 women are CEOs in the Fortune 500.

Of course, the absence of women from the boards of most companies may be less to do with male bias and more to do with this cold fact: there is a correlation between the proportion of women on the board and the weaker financial performance of the company. Now this might be because men make better accountants – though I doubt it – and however many accountants companies have (and the UK has proportionately more accountants than any other major competitor; the US has more lawyers), they do not seem to have saved many companies from the financial crisis of 2008. Instead, we need to focus on the word 'correlation' and distinguish it from causation, because the direction of cause is critical here, as Figure 14 suggests.

What this figure implies is that women are appointed only when conditions are much worse than those that generally prevail for men's appointments – which means that the task for women is much more difficult and that we can correlate poor performance with women – but it is the poor performance causing the appointment of women not the other way around. Indeed, in terms of performance of companies after appointment, there is

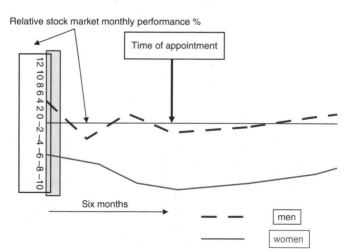

Relative stock market monthly performance %

Time of appointment

Six months

men

women

14. **Women on the board and performance**

proportionately little difference between men and women in many studies, though some suggest that gender diversity is positively correlated with success – at least provided the women on the board are well qualified, and Keohane notes that centuries of exclusion have provided women with a different set of questions to ask of our leaders.

What should be done about the lack of diversity amongst our leaders? Well, that depends upon where you sit. If you are a THWaMP who wants to maintain that position, then clearly nothing needs to be done. But if you think something needs changing, then it still depends upon what you think the source of the problem is. Figure 15 reproduces Alvesson and Billing's typology that addresses the issue of gender imbalance. Box 1 represents those people who assume that the genders are similar and that something should be done for ethical reasons. This often leads to a legislative approach, such as that undertaken by the

Concern for Ethical/Political Issues

Gender Similarities		Gender Differences
1. Equal Opportunities Unjust to discriminate Legislation required	**2.** Alternative Values Unbridgeable differences Alternative organizations	
3. Meritocracy Inefficient to discriminate Enlightened self-interest	**4.** Special Contribution Different but complementary Women more appropriate	

Concern for Organizational Efficiency

15. **Gender: cause and effect**

Norwegian government that was mentioned before. Box 2 follows the same ethical line but suggests that the genders are essentially different and thus no legislative change can make any difference. The only real solution here is for women to set up alternative organizations, and indeed the proportion of new businesses set up by women does seem to be increasing as some women perceive the glass ceiling of traditional male-dominated organizations as impenetrable. Box 3 takes the genders to be essentially similar, but takes an efficiency rather than an ethical approach and argues that this makes the case for a meritocratic approach to save 'wasting' the talent of women. Last, Box 4 is efficiency-oriented but assumes the genders are different and focuses on the way women can make a 'special contribution' to organizations.

Now the point here is to recognize the connection between the explanation and the prescription, because this explains why different strategies for change are suggested – and, if they fail, why opponents of the strategy then try to reframe the problem in a different category. In fact, we wouldn't expect there to be much difference between men and women because the genders are not markedly different in general measures of intelligence, nor in personality traits, and, if anything, women in Western Europe and North America are more often better qualified than their male counterparts. It would seem that the most important factors for explaining the differential success are actually the mundane features of asymmetric domestic responsibilities, sex discrimination, and gendered assumptions, and the stronger work networks of men that secure better access to more challenging positions and to better jobs. In effect, women (who tend to have stronger social networks than men) are expected to be more compassionate as leaders than men – and when they are, this behaviour is regarded as less robust than the more aggressive leadership expected of men. Of course, some women leaders adopt a more aggressive style, but these actions are often regarded as 'inappropriate'. Either way, the odds are stacked against women leaders.

Of course, this also provides ammunition for those 'I told you so' moments, because we seem to make instant decisions about leaders or their strategies so that if we support them and they are subsequently successful, well, we knew they would be. And if they fail, well the situation must have changed, or someone must have undermined them, or some other excuse. This is not new. There is already a lot of evidence to suggest that instant responses to leaders (positive or negative) are very common. The selection of officers for the US Army during the First World War was premised on similar stereotypes: those applicants who were perceived to have attractive aspects – either in terms of the veritable THWaMP variety or mere 'attractive personalities' – were deemed to be more intelligent, more courageous, and more (suitably) aggressive. Or, as Edward Lee Thorndike put it, a 'halo effect' (or 'devil effect' for less attractive recruits) was created in an instant, and this distorted people's assumptions about their entire character and potential.

We might consider where the competency models fit into all this. Many competency models are configured on the basis of analysing the competencies of existing leaders. These are then distilled into a manageable list and recruitment methods are then moulded around the required competency frameworks. But note what this does: it takes an existing group of leaders and attributes their success on the basis of competencies that are allegedly important in generating the success. For those of you who smell a circular argument in here, you have found one. What we actually need to do is compare groups of successful and unsuccessful leaders, or leaders and followers, and then see what is different about the (successful) leaders and trace the causal connections to success. Otherwise, we don't know whether what we have is correlations or causations. It may be, as we have already seen, that being a THWaMP is correlated with successful organizations, and it may well be that being a THWaMP is a prerequisite for successful organizations – but it may equally be that successful organizations simply recruit people who are THWaMPs. So unless we can be certain that the existing competency framework really is the cause of success (or failure), we should be very wary of going down this path.

This would not matter quite so much if we already had a very diverse leadership that reflected the population – it would simply mean that diverse organizations would keep reproducing their own bias and thus the diversity would persist – but not change. However, since organizations tend to be led by THWaMPs, we can look forward to getting more THWaMPs in the next generation of leaders. Is this just a case of selecting in your own image, or is there another reason?

Social identity theory

If we consider the utility of social identity theory, we might get a glimpse of an alternative explanation. This approach suggests that we always tend to place other people in categories that are either favourable, because they support our own identity, or unfavourable, because they are deemed to be different from us. This identification process is both individually and group-oriented, so that under certain conditions we perceive individuals as representatives of groups, not as unique characters. Indeed, personal identity – the 'I' – does not exist in isolation from social identity – the 'we'. Once categorized the theory then suggests that we constitute differences within the in-group (us) as smaller than those between the in-group and the out-group (them). Furthermore, the in-group's norms and stereotypes (which are largely favourable) lead to specific comparators to ensure self-enhancement. For example, young girls living on a run-down council estate are likely to view supermodels not as better than themselves but as unable to survive in such a tough environment – thus the comparator reproduces the self-enhancing social identity of the girls.

Furthermore, this whole process generates *prototypes* that emulate the social identity of the group and *depersonalize* its members, who appear so similar they become interchangeable: we expect to agree with each other on group-related issues, we tend to support emergent group norms, and we advance the interests of the group above our own personal interests. In effect, 'we' perceive ourselves as all alike in our positive attributions and perceive 'them' as essentially identical in our negative perceptions about them. This serves to reduce any uncertainty we have about ourselves, our status, our likely behaviour, and it does the same for 'them'.

Such prototypes are seldom so clearly articulated that we would expect people to be able to write them down in an agreed list; indeed, they are likely to change in time and space as the context changes and to become more important as group membership becomes more important – often in response to an external threat. The consequence for leadership is that those group members who are closest to the group prototype are likely to have most influence – to become and remain the leaders as long as the conditions continue. Since this influence relates to the prototype, not the individual (though it appears otherwise to the group members), that implies that changing conditions generate different prototypes, and this explains why prototypical icons can suddenly seem to lose influence. For example, Churchill was regarded by many of the British as a belligerent and dangerous maverick in the 1930s, but as perfectly encapsulating the self-perceived prototypical character of the British under threat – a stoic bulldog in the face of great danger – hence his popularity and rise to pre-eminence as prime minister. However, once the war was over his character – which had not changed – was perceived to be out of kilter with the requirements of the post-war world. For that, the more congenial and inclusive character of Clement Attlee was the required prototypical leader.

Prototypicality, then, depends upon contextual stability, though as was suggested in Chapter 2, the framing and reframing of 'situations' is part of the armoury of any leader. Nonetheless, there are several techniques that leaders used to prolong their control which feed into the prototyping model:

- Accentuate the existing prototype – be more like one of 'us' than embody some 'superior' traits or appear like one of 'them'.

- Seek out and attack in-group deviants – this is the point where dissent, constructive or otherwise, is reframed as the action of 'traitors'.

- Demonize the out-group to deflect attention from internal problems.

- Stand up for the group – demonstrate favouritism to in-group members rather than fairness between groups.

The leader, therefore, is likely to be the in-group prototype:

- The person most representative of shared social identity.

- The person who exemplifies what in-group members have in common – maximum intra-group similarity; and exemplifies what makes them different from the comparative out-group – maximum inter-group difference.

- The person who makes 'us' feel different from – and better than – 'them'.

The riots in Iran in June 2009 and in the Xinjiang province of China in July 2009 are good examples of how this approach makes sense of the decisions of leaders under duress. This also explains why 'groupthink' (the tendency for groups to suppress internal dissent) is prevalent amongst groups under pressure and why minorities and non-prototypical individuals and groups find it so difficult to break into leadership positions within established organizations and institutions.

That doesn't mean it's impossible, but it does mean it's very difficult. In fact, when a crisis breaks out, the position of the prototype leader is usually strengthened. For example, Gordon Brown's position as Prime Minister of the UK was under immense threat in the summer of 2008 as he struggled to demonstrate an alternative vision for the post-Blair Labour Party. But as soon as the financial crisis hit in the autumn of 2008, all thoughts of displacing him were dropped as the Party pulled together and it sought the protection of the person with the most prototypical character required in a financial crisis – the dour, responsible, serious face of the ex-Chancellor of the Exchequer: Gordon Brown. Yet ironically, nine months later, when the same British Prime Minister again faced significant rebellions as the expenses scandal broke within Parliament, he failed to act as the fiscal 'witchfinder general', and thus allowed the scapegoat hunt so common when uncertainty descends and we seek a resolution by concentrating blame upon the individual leader – Gordon Brown.

But success for prototypical leaders depends not just on persuading 'us' that we are different from and better than 'them', but also on persuading 'me' and 'you' to become 'us'. Luckily for leaders, that need not be that difficult because it depends not upon rational analysis of 'the facts' but upon an emotional and often unconscious response. In fact, all that is required is Benedict Anderson's 'leap of imagination'. What he meant by that was that since we could never really know whether other people were really like 'us', or like 'them', we simply had to imagine one or other was the case. Thus, it did not matter that the soldiers on both sides of the trenches in the First World War actually had more in common with each other than with their respective leaders in terms of quality of life, income, habits, and so on. What mattered was that 'they' were obviously very different from 'us', and that turned 'you' and 'me' sufficiently into 'us' to want to fight 'them'.

We can see this in action in the construction of British and French identity, for there are good grounds to suggest that until the war between the revolutionary French army under Napoleon and the British, under Wellington, it may be that most people in Britain regarded themselves as English or Scottish or Welsh or Irish – but not British. Similarly, the 'French' might have considered themselves to be Breton or Norman or whatever region they came from – but not French (indeed, most people in France at the time did not speak French but a regional language). However, the war catapulted the two nations against each other, and the collision propelled Napoleon and Wellington to leadership positions not just as generals but as prototypes for their own 'new' nations. Thus, we can read the literature at the time as pitting two prototype leaders against each other who are representative of their own nation. Napoleon and Wellington are not perceived as two individuals doing similar jobs, but as two encapsulations of diametrically opposed nationalities – which are formed in the crucible of war. The lists of character words below represent how these two individuals and countries came to be identified with one side against the other.

Let us return to the beginning of this chapter to conclude. We began by looking at Warren Harding as a popular but ineffective leader and the role of first impressions that generate halos which bias our interpretation of leaders. That implies that we need to be very careful about the issues of micro-leadership. By that, I mean we perhaps put too much emphasis on the rational aspects of

Wellington	Napoleon
Private	Public
Dogged	Imaginative
Logistics	Strategy
Gentleman	Upstart
Graft	Gifted
Freedom	Equality
Stability	Instability
Caution	Risk
Troops as 'scum'	Troops as 'family'
Pragmatist	Centralist
Book-keeper	Shooting star

leadership – the vision, the policies, the experience that leaders bring – and not enough emphasis on the emotional aspects of leading – the way people interpret very small acts, sayings, glances, body language, and so on. Of course, there is a whole raft of writing on emotional intelligence – and there are many different definitions of the term – but we should be aware that people with high emotional intelligence are not morally superior to those without high emotional intelligence. Hitler, for example, was extraordinarily effective in manipulating people's emotions, but this does not make him objectively moral. Moreover, it is because emotions are such a powerful motivator that we ought to limit their significance – that, after all, is the reason for living according to a system of laws rather than at the whim of a tyrant whose emotional intelligence is a liability for all who disagree with the tyrant. Nevertheless, we are more enamoured of leaders who remember our names and who feel like one of us than of leaders who never deign to say hello to us but have astute policies for dealing with a world so complex we don't even pretend to understand it or them. Indeed, they are not like 'us' at all; they are more like 'them'.

Chapter 6
How do leaders lead?

On traits, Scrooge, and koi carp

You may recall from Chapter 3 that Thomas Carlyle figured as one of the first 'modern' leadership scholars with his 'Great Men' approach. But why does this approach still remain popular despite its limited empirical support and theoretical weakness? Well, one reason is that many of us still hanker after simple solutions to complex problems: when the credit crunch starts to unhinge the entire economic infrastructure, rather than think through the complexity of the issues, we prefer to find a scapegoat (we shall return to this phenomenon in the next chapter). Looking for heroes (and villains) also enables us to avoid responsibility and to maintain an infantilist approach to leaders that may well have originated with our childhood relationships to parents or equivalent authority figures.

Nonetheless, by the end of the Second World War, the early trait theories that had evolved in response to the problem of officer selection for the military during war time had begun to pose alternatives to the 'Great Men' theory. These early theories suggested that leaders do have special traits/qualities that distinguish them from non-leaders and these seem to be:

- talkativeness;
- intelligence – providing the gap between leader and followers was not too wide;
- initiative and willingness to take responsibility;
- self-confidence; and
- sociability.

But it soon became apparent that these traits needed to be contextualized if they were to be regarded as important to leadership. Indeed, it also became clear that many studies that produced negative correlations remained unpublished, biasing the whole area. Despite the fact that each study (rather like contemporary competence models) generated markedly different traits, the assumption persists that if only we look hard enough, we will discover the proverbial golden ticket – the *really true* list of traits. But since we seldom match successful with unsuccessful leaders, and since we seldom have incontrovertible evidence that the action of leaders makes an objectively measurable impact upon organizational performance, we are still left with two problems.

First, are the tests for competence objective? For example, the intelligence-testing system that processed civilians into various units of the American armed services during the Second World War were as fallible as any educational or other intellectual test: they suggested that one-quarter of all those tested were illiterate, while half the whites and 90% of the African Americans had a mental age below 13 years. Since the tests involved questions such as 'Scrooge was a character in which of the following: *Vanity Fair*, *A Christmas Carol*, *Romola* or *Henry IV*?' and 'What is the term for spatial perspective in Renaissance art?', we can rest assured that scientific and cultural objectivity was never a strong point in them. But the practical consequences were to keep most African American soldiers out of direct combat units until late in the war.

Second, we haven't even looked at the followers yet. What happens if we have a fantastically talented leader – in terms of traits – but a group of subordinates who have absolutely no interest in following that leader? So here's the other problem: traits manifest themselves as possessions of an individual but leadership is a relationship. This is a bit like buying the best koi carp in the commercial aquarium but forgetting that you don't have a pond to put it in.

Behavioural/style approaches

While the Allied forces were busy constructing list of traits to select their officers, Kurt Lewin, having escaped from Nazi Germany himself, was beginning a set of experiments to see whether the behaviour of the leader, rather than his or her traits, made any difference to organizational success. In his famous 'Boys' Club Experiments', Lewin concluded that boys (followers) would generally comply with authoritarian leaders when the latter were present but avoid work when the latter were absent. In contrast, leaders who adopted a *laissez-faire* approach got little work out of the boys when present or absent, while the democratic leaders managed to get (roughly) half the boys to work productively whether they were present or not. The conclusion was that democratic leaders generate the highest level of satisfaction amongst followers – but note that the most productive followers are those coerced by a present authoritarian.

This division between satisfaction and productivity has formed the basis for many studies ever since. The University of Michigan studies suggested that leaders were either *production-oriented* – where followers were perceived as factors of production, as means to an end; or they were *employee-oriented* – where followers were perceived as a key resource. Investigations into aircrew behaviour by Ohio State University then reproduced this basic task/people dichotomy (though they called it 'initiating structure' and 'consideration') and concluded that leaders could undertake both activities rather than choose one or the other. Blake and Mouton managed to capture this dichotomy well in their 'managerial grid',

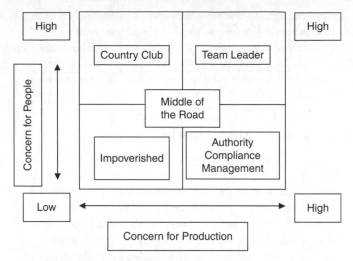

16. Blake and Mouton's managerial grid

which is reproduced in Figure 16. Here leaders could either be disengaged from the task and the people and demonstrate an 'impoverished' style; or they could show high concern for the people but not for the task – as if they were leading a Country Club which existed just for the benefit of the members; or they could be solely focused on the task at the expense of the people – an authority compliance style of management; they could, of course, sit in the middle of the graph, or, finally, they could show high concern for task and people and operate as 'team leader'. Interestingly, this grid has prevailed in popularity since its first inception in the mid-1960s, but it has yet to generate significant empirical support for its key assumption that team leaders were possible and optimal.

Contingency theory

At the same time that the managerial grid was taking off, another shift in approach became apparent as the focus moved from the choice of style by leaders (task or people) to the importance of the context in determining which style would actually work – this was the beginning of contingency theory.

Fred Fiedler began this move with his 'least preferred co-worker' approach that retained the task/relationship dichotomy. Fiedler assumed that leaders were either task- or relationship-oriented and could not change, but the effectiveness of orientation depended upon the favourableness of the situation. This, in turn, was defined by:

- The leader's *position power* – the leader's legitimate authority to evaluate and reward performance, to punish errors, and demote group members;

- The *structure* of the team's task – the number and clarity of rules, regulations, and procedures for getting work done: the higher the structure, the higher the leader's control;

- *Leader–member* relationships: either positive or negative.

These variables, in turn, would generate favourable situations, or unfavourable, or moderate situations.

Favourable leadership situations comprised:

- task highly structured;
- considerable position power;
- good leader–member relationships.

Here, the group expected to be told what to do and did not expect consultation, so task-oriented leadership worked best.

Unfavourable leadership situations comprised:

- unstructured task;
- little position power;
- poor leader–member relationships.

Here again, the group expected to be told what to do and did not expect consultation, so (again) task-oriented leadership worked best. Only in moderate situations – which sat between the favourable and unfavourable so that leaders had moderate power, moderate support, and a complex task – was consultation necessary to secure buy-in, and here, and only here, relationship-oriented leadership was best.

So what happens when leaders find themselves in the 'wrong' situation? Well, since leaders cannot change their orientation – according to Fiedler – all they could do was attempt to change the situation. And why was this? Why should followers need task leadership when the situation was either favourable or unfavourable? Fiedler's response was that not all of this was explicable; there was indeed a 'black box' at work, so that we did not know why it worked but it worked. Well, it worked up to a point: at least the situation was now in the spotlight – so we had a pond for our koi carp – and it implied that perhaps it was difficult for leaders to be successful in all situations. But it isn't clear that a personality profile can predict behaviour, let alone leadership success, and we still do not seem to be too concerned with the nature of the followers or their relationship with the leaders. Moreover, as we saw in Chapter 2, part of the success of leaders is rooted in their ability to reframe 'situations' so that they appear differently and are thus open to different approaches.

Hersey and Blanchard's 'situational leadership theory' certainly acknowledged that multiple variables do exist in leadership, but argued that leaders could not possibly hope to cope with such a high level of complexity. Therefore they should concentrate on the most important one – the relationship between leader and followers – because if the followers decide not to follow, everything else is irrelevant. This then led them to suggest that the leader's behaviour should be adjusted to the maturity level of the followers – which changes over time and tended to proceed along the following trajectory:

1) *Unable and unwilling* – least mature: telling/directing leadership style.
2) *Unable but willing*: selling/coaching leadership style.
3) *Able but unwilling*: participating/supporting leadership style.
4) *Able and willing* – most mature: delegating leadership style.

This has proved to be one of the most successful models in the executive market: it is intuitive, simple, and easy to understand – but again, it has very little empirical support for its validity. One reason is that the model implies a concern for an aggregate level of follower maturity that perhaps does not exist; in other words, that followers embody different levels of responsibility and do not merely reflect a composite norm. Another is that it isn't really clear what they mean by 'maturity' – does that relate to confidence, skill, effort, motivation, quiescence? And if so, what are the weights attached to these variations? Moreover, whose interpretation of follower maturity are we using here: leaders' or followers'? And what about leaders' (im)maturity – who said they were outside this equation?

For 'leader–member exchange theory' (LMX), or as it was originally and enticingly labelled, 'vertical linkage dyad (VLD) theory', leaders don't develop an 'average' relationship with followers, instead they establish different relationships with each subordinate, but over time these fall into two distinct groups, each formed through the initial action of the leader. For the in-group, the leader provides increased autonomy and responsibility on unstructured tasks, and if the group responds positively, then further reciprocal action confirms this group as the equivalent of the sheriff's 'deputies'. But if the leader does not offer similar possibilities to other subordinates, or if they are perceived by the leader to respond unconstructively, over time they become an 'out-group', the equivalent of 'hired hands' rather than deputies. This group relates to the leader on a purely contractual (or transactional) basis: they turn up at work, do the minimum, get paid, go home, and forget about work. However, if they lose the stress of responsibility at work that falls upon the in-group, they nevertheless suffer from stress via the uncertainty of their employment – since they will be the first to lose their jobs.

Once more, an intuitive approach has, as yet, only marginal empirical support for its claims, and it may be that resentment of those in the out-group cancels out the benefits of developing a better relationship with the in-group. Moreover, as we saw in the previous chapter, the constructing of an out-group that embodies few of the characteristics associated with the prototyping of the in-group, while often counter-productive for the effectiveness of the overall organization, might actually be a 'normal' response of groups, if not an inevitable aspect of social life. So, for leaders, is the real trick to try to tip-toe around all these problem areas while at the same time mobilizing as many of the group members as possible?

Possibly, and perhaps the most sophisticated of contingency approaches is that associated with the path–goal theory of Robert House. Here, the leader's task was to smooth the followers' path to the collective goal by removing roadblocks and facilitating motivation using one of four leader behaviour styles:

1) Directive leaders, who would communicate expectations and require rule following to complete scheduled work to clear performance standards.

2) Supportive leaders, who expressed concern for followers' needs and welfare and created a climate that demonstrated support and generated mutual respect.

3) Participative leaders, who shared decision-making authority with followers.

4) Achievement–oriented leaders, who set challenging goals and expected very high levels of performance.

In turn, the leader's influence was contingent upon two sets of variables: the work environment (situation), comprising the task structure, the work group, and the authority system; and the followers, comprising their ability level (and perceptions of these), their attitude towards authoritarianism, their need for affiliation, their need for structure, and their locus of control (those with a strong internal locus of control believe that events are controlled by themselves and prefer participative leadership; those with a strong external locus of control believe that events are determined by fate or luck or others and prefer directive leadership).

The model's causal explanation was derived from expectancy theory which perceived motivation as a rational choice on the effort level given:

1) the likelihood of achieving task (expectancy),
2) the likelihood of receiving beneficial reward (valence), and
3) the likelihood of avoiding undesirable outcome.

In this approach, any leader could exhibit any style, or combination of styles – so it is not a trait approach but an adaptive behavioural approach. However, there is an assumed tendency – most people have preferred styles that may, or may not, fit the requirements of the situation. If, by now, you are starting to drown in the number of variables involved, a diagrammatic lifebelt is given in Figure 17.

The implication of all this is that the leader's behaviour should match the requirements of the follower and situational characteristics, and he or she should select the appropriate leader behaviour style to help followers achieve their goals. Thus:

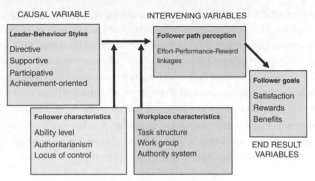

CAUSAL VARIABLE   INTERVENING VARIABLES

Leader-Behaviour Styles

Directive
Supportive
Participative
Achievement-oriented

Follower path perception

Effort-Performance-Reward
linkages

Follower goals

Satisfaction
Rewards
Benefits

END RESULT
VARIABLES

Follower characteristics

Ability level
Authoritarianism
Locus of control

Workplace characteristics

Task structure
Work group
Authority system

SITUATIONAL MODERATOR VARIABLES

17. **Path–goal theory**

- ambiguous tasks require directive leadership to reduce uncertainty and to increase the probability and desirability of the outcome;

- stressful, boring, tedious, or dangerous environments require supportive leadership, which increases self-confidence and reduces anxiety so as to increase the probability and desirability of the outcome;

- when followers were ready for empowerment, then participative leadership was required; and

- when followers had high achievement-orientations, then achievement-oriented leadership was appropriate.

This seems relatively intuitive – so what's the catch? Well, the catch is threefold. First, the accumulation of so many variables renders the task virtually impossible: if we were able to obtain an objective score for each of the variables involved, by the time we had accumulated the data, the situation would probably have changed beyond recognition. Second, even this implies that we can secure a degree of objectivity in the measurement of human behaviour, but that seems to have eluded us. Third, it may be that followers actually want very similar things from their leaders – they want to be recognized and protected. The problem is that leaders – and of course almost all leaders are also followers at different levels in the hierarchy – recognize a different 'reality'. Leaders tend to realize that completion of the task is critical and, while leaders may be concerned for followers, the leaders' upward-looking (task-related) gaze is perceived by followers as disinterest in them. And the irony is that these very same 'disinterested' leaders often believe their own leaders exhibit a similar lack of interest in their followers. Does this general tendency also explain why followers respond differently to charismatic leaders?

Charismatic leadership

Charisma is a 'divinely bestowed power or talent' and its etymological origins lie in the Greek word *Kharisma*, from *kharis:* 'divine grace' or 'favour'. In fact, most people now use the term to mean someone extraordinary, with a quality or authority that influences or inspires large numbers of people. For Max Weber, the German sociologist who wrote the seminal text on charisma, these were people whose authority was beyond the understanding of most people and who were very rare. Hence Weber's version of charisma – what I shall call 'strong charisma' – is not about people with strong personalities but people who can mobilize their followers in some magical way. It was fundamentally an irrational and emotional phenomenon and its bearers had a 'calling', a ruthless dedication to achieve a goal. That might also explain why charismatic leaders are predominantly men – because times of crisis, often associated with war of some kind, usually favour those in command of the military, who have been and still are predominantly men. Of the well-known female charismatics – Boudicca, Jean d'Arc, and Elizabeth I, for example – all are associated with military combat. Jean d'Arc, for example, is not only associated with the military defeat of the English but also with a masculine appearance.

Weber carved out a conceptual space for charismatic leadership by differentiating power from authority – the latter was always legitimate in the eyes of the followers, the former need not be – and by distinguishing three different kinds of authority. Traditional authority occurred when followers followed because they had always done so – perhaps the followers of monarchs represent this best; rational-legal authority, best known as bureaucracy, where followers followed because it was rational for them to do so, rather than because they had always done so; and charismatic authority. But charismatics were unique in the ability to attract followers who were devoted to the person's transcendent powers that seemed to provide the possibility of a radical and hitherto unknown solution to some kind of social crisis. In fact, Weber's examples are almost all religious leaders, and he makes great play of their calling, their destiny, which is manifest in the display of miracles and in their fulfilment of prophecies. For Weber, charismatic leadership was the only form of 'non-coercive authority' – though it is questionable to assume that the choice between heaven and everlasting hell is a non-coercive choice. Moreover, because the charisma was embodied within an individual, it usually died out with that individual or became routinized through an institution, such as the Church.

Just because Weber's charismatics were extraordinary mobilizers of followers did not mean they were necessarily revolutionary, indeed, they could be reactionary, seeking to return a society to a previous state, but more often than not they were both – they tried to regain the past but only by proceeding to a new future. There is an important lesson in here for change leadership. So often we assume that change is about going forward and leaving the past behind, but Weber's account implies that success relates to a Janus-like ability to do both. Take the 1933 German election as an illustration. While the conservative parties harked back to the good old days, the ruling social democrats ran the equivalent of an 'it doesn't get any better' campaign, and the communists looked steadfastly towards the utopian future. Only the Nazis combined all three perspectives: Germany could regain the glory of before, but not by going backwards, not by staying put, and certainly not by abandoning the past for some mystical communist alternative future. Instead, this would require rejecting the present, avoiding the communist future, and reigniting the past glories by bringing their essence into an alternative Nazi future. Thus Weber's charismatics – and he had warned that a charismatic might well undermine the rational legal German world – were often conservative revolutionaries, intent on 'reclaiming the past from the present during moments of distress'.

This emotional groundswell of supporters also implies that charisma was a deeply destabilizing and itself unstable force. To some degree, followers could share their leader's charisma by joining his or her organization – though how long this would last depended upon whether the charismatic could continue to pull off notable miracles at will. We can see precisely this characteristic when we consider how political leaders, celebrities, football managers, radio presenters, and so on are hailed as god's gift one day and then condemned to symbolic (and occasionally actual) death the next day.

It's also worth considering how desperately people want to believe in the ability of charismatic leaders to save them in times of acute distress, and how, when we do not have such crises to hand, we invent them in films and novels (such as the *Harry Potter* series, *The Lord of the Rings*, and suchlike), as if our own existence is not just mundane but unbearably ordinary. For these very same reasons, many people who are involved in military combat often hark back to their 'glory days' when the 'sting of battle' literally enthralled them. Perhaps for these reasons, charismatics often believe themselves to be the bearers of a destiny designed by others. As Churchill noted on taking office in 1940: 'This cannot be accident, it must be design. I was kept for this job.' Charisma might also explain Lord Acton's dictum, in a letter to Bishop Mandell

Creighton (1887), that 'Power tends to corrupt, and absolute power corrupts absolutely. Great men are almost always bad men.'

If Weber concentrated upon the extraordinary nature of what I have called 'strong' charisma, many scholars since have argued that his concepts cannot be operationalized and are used in a binary format – either you are charismatic or you are not, and there is no argument about the categorization. Instead, many have opted to see charisma as a continuum that is closer to extrovert personality rather than the superhumans that Weber was concerned with. In these accounts of (weak) charisma, the relationship between individual (leader) and followers is based upon deeply held and shared ideological (not material) values, where the charismatics accomplish unusual (rather than miraculous) feats through followers who are exceptionally loyal to, and have a high degree of trust in, their leader. In these circumstances, the followers are willing to make personal sacrifices in the interests of the collective vision, and permanent crises are as unnecessary as permanent miracles.

This bears an uncanny resemblance to transformational leadership, as originally developed by MacGregor Burns, who differentiated this from both charismatic and transactional leadership. For MacGregor Burns, transactional leadership was restricted to an exchange relationship between leader and follower – though whether that exchange was economic (such as wages), or social (such as promotion), or psychological (such as friendship), was less relevant than that it was an exchange, it was very common, and it was very limited in its effects. In contrast, transformational leadership was not an exchange process at all but occurred when transformational leaders appealed to followers' values beyond their personal interests. Of course, it may be that charismatics also have an exchange relationship with their followers but one based on an exchange of identity. However, this ability to lift the vision of followers from the everyday to the extraordinary required charisma, but not all charismatics were transformational. For

MacGregor Burns, charismatics who were not transformational were 'power-wielders', that is, leaders who secured a commitment from followers that satisfied the leaders', rather than the followers', interests. Finally, power-wielders tended to induce high levels of dependency amongst their followers, while transformational leaders appeared to operate along the reverse principle, empowering not disempowering their followers; securing adherence to a body of ideals not allegiance to an ideal body.

Many have followed in MacGregor Burns's footsteps, with Zaleznik differentiating between psychologically 'healthy' and 'unhealthy' leaders, while Howell preferred to differentiate between 'socialized' and 'personalized' leaders, and Bass contrasted 'authentic' with inauthentic, or 'pseudo-transformational', leaders. The problem seems to me that all of these divisions are rooted in the subjective ethics of the observer – since we don't approve of particular leaders, we label them as unhealthy or inauthentic and so on. But this is to miss the point of charisma: it doesn't matter whether academic observers are unswayed by the siren calls of religious fanatics or political monsters, what matters is whether followers are swayed by them. Under these circumstances, the point is not to ignore the ethical dimension of charismatic leadership, but to ask ourselves whether followers believe their charismatic leader is acting ethically.

This also means we need to be very wary of charismatic leaders. They may be important in a crisis, but may be impelled to maintain the crisis if resolving it undermines their authority. They may achieve extraordinary levels of mobilization – but it may not always be for causes with which we might agree. And they may prove critical in breaking the logjam of indecision – but when they have gone, are their achievements sustainable or do their very actions as gifted individuals undermine the possibility of sustainable action by the many? In the next chapter, I want to look at the latter, the followers – do they have a role in all this, and if so, what is it?

Chapter 7
What about the followers?

The English word 'follower' is derived from the Old English word *Folgian* and the Old Norse *Fylgja*, meaning to accompany, help, or, ironically, to lead. These first three definitions are relatively positive:

1) An ordinary person who accepts the leadership of another.
2) Someone who travels behind or pursues another.
3) One who follows; a pursuer, an attendant, a disciple, a dependent associate, a retainer.

However, the negative images of 'follower' are more clearly visible in these definitions:

4) A person or algorithm that compensates for lack of sophistication or native stupidity by efficiently following some simple procedure shown to have been effective in the past.
5) A sweetheart, a Trollope.
6) (Steam engine) The removable flange of a piston.
7) The part of a machine that receives motion from another.
8) Gaelic: Surname ending in 'agh' or 'augh' = 'follower of' – Cavanagh = 'follower of Kevin'.

Those readers familiar with the British comedian Harry Enfield's character 'Kevin' – a teenage nightmare of sullenness and irresponsibility – will note the diminution of the role of follower in the light of the superordinate 'leader'. Indeed, when listing the traits required by formal leaders, it is usual for a class to come up with any number of characteristics: charisma, energy, vision, confidence, tolerance, communication skills, 'presence', the ability to multi-task, listening skills, decisiveness, team-building, 'distance', strategic skills, and so on and so forth. No two lists constructed by leadership students, or leaders, ever seems to be the same, and no consensus exists as to which traits or characteristics or competencies are essential or optional. Indeed, the most interesting aspect of list-making is that by the time the list is complete, the only plausible description of the owner of such a skill base is 'god'. Irrespective of whether the traits are contradictory, it is usually impossible for anyone to name leaders who have all these traits, at least to any significant degree; yet it seems clear that all these traits are necessary to a successful organization. Thus we are left with a paradox: the leaders who have all of these – the omniscient leaders – do not exist, but we seem to need them. Indeed, complaints about leaders and calls for more or better leadership occur on such a regular basis that one would be forgiven for assuming that there was a time when good leaders were ubiquitous. Sadly, a trawl through the leadership archives reveals no golden past, but nevertheless a pervasive yearning for such an era. An urban myth like this 'romance of leadership' – the era when heroic leaders were allegedly plentiful and solved all our problems – is not only misconceived but positively counter-productive because it sets up a model of leadership that few, if any of us, can ever match, and thus it inhibits the development of leadership, warts and all. It should be no surprise, then, to see, for example, the continuous re-advertising of vacancies for head teachers when the possibilities of success are either beyond the control of individuals or so clearly defined by comparative reference to Superman and Wonderwoman that only those who can walk on water need apply: not for these leaders the Roman warning: *nemo sine vitio est* (no-one is without fault).

The traditional solution to this kind of recruitment problem, or the perceived weakness of contemporary business chief executives or directors of public services or not-for-profit organizations, is to demand better recruitment criteria so that the 'weak' are selected out, leaving the 'strong' to save the day. But this is to reproduce the problem not to solve it. An alternative approach might be to start from where we are, not where we would like to be: with all leaders – because they are human – as flawed individuals, not all leaders as the embodiments of all that we merely mortal and imperfect followers would like them to be: perfect. The former approach resembles a 'white elephant' – in both dictionary definitions: as a mythical beast that is itself a deity, and as an expensive and foolhardy endeavour. Indeed, in Thai history, the king would give an albino elephant to his least favoured noble because the special dietary and religious requirements would ruin the noble.

The white elephant is also a manifestation of Plato's approach to leadership, for to him the most important question was 'Who

18. The white elephant

should lead us?' The answer, of course, was the wisest amongst us: the individual with the greatest knowledge, skill, power, resources of all kinds. This kind of approach echoes our current search criteria for omniscient leaders and leads us unerringly to select charismatics, larger-than-life characters, and personalities whose magnetic charm, astute vision, and personal forcefulness will displace all the bland and miserable failures that we have previously recruited to that position – though strangely enough using precisely the same selection criteria. Unless the new leaders are indeed Platonic philosopher-kings, endowed with extraordinary wisdom, they will surely fail sooner or later, and then the whole circus will start again, probably with the same result.

Of course, for Plato, it was more than likely that the leaders would be men; after all, Greek women were not even citizens of their own city-states, though Plato did admit that it was theoretically possible that a woman might have all the natural requirements of leadership. Since Plato's time, assumptions about the role of gender in leadership have varied enormously, even if the presence of women as leaders has proved remarkably limited and remarkably stable (see Chapter 5).

An alternative approach is to start from the inherent weakness of leaders and work to inhibit and restrain this, rather than to assume it will not occur. Karl Popper provides a firmer foundation for this in his assumption that, just as we can only disprove rather than prove scientific theories, so we should adopt mechanisms that inhibit leaders rather than surrender ourselves to them. For Popper, democracy was an institutional mechanism for deselecting leaders, rather than a benefit in and of itself, and, even though there are precious few democratic systems operating within non-political organizations, similar processes ought to be replicable elsewhere. Otherwise, although omniscient leaders are a figment of irresponsible followers' minds and utopian recruiters' fervid imaginations, when subordinates question their leader's direction or skill these (in)subordinates are usually replaced by those 'more aligned with the current strategic thinking' – otherwise known as 'yes-people'. In turn, such subordinates become transformed into irresponsible followers whose advice to their leader is often limited to destructive consent: they may know that their leader is wrong, but there are all kinds of reasons not to say as much, hence they consent to the destruction of their own leader and possibly their own organization too.

Popper's warnings about leaders, however, suggest that it is the responsibility of followers to inhibit leaders' errors and to remain as constructive dissenters, helping the organization achieve its goals but not allowing any leaders to undermine this. Thus constructive dissenters attribute the assumptions of Socratic ignorance rather than Platonic knowledge to their leaders: they know that nobody is omniscient and act accordingly.

Of course, for this to work, subordinates need to remain committed to the goals of the community or organization (and of course, there are often good reasons not be committed to an organization that has no reciprocal commitment to you) while simultaneously retaining their spirit of independence from the whims of their leaders. It is this paradoxical combination of commitment

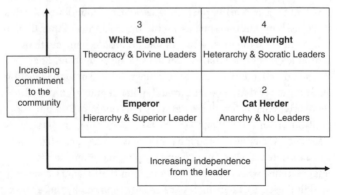

19. **Leadership, followership, commitment, and independence**

and independence that provides the most fertile ground for responsible followers. Figure 19 outlines the possible combinations of this mix of commitment and independence. Again, this is for illustrative purposes and generates a series of Weberian 'ideal types' that are neither 'ideal' in any normative sense nor 'typical' in any universal sense. On the contrary, these types are for heuristic purposes, designed to flag up and magnify the extreme consequences of theoretically polar positions.

Despite these reservations, Box 1 – the hierarchy – probably contains the most typical form of relationship between leaders and followers, wherein a conventional hierarchy functions under a leader deemed to be superior to his or her followers by dint of the conducive *personal* qualities of intelligence, vision, charisma, and so on and so forth, and thus to be responsible for solving all the problems of the organization. Such imperial ambitions resonate with the label for this form of leader: the emperor. In turn, that generates followers who are only marginally committed to the organization's goals – often because these are reduced to the personal goals of the leader – and hence the followers remain literally 'irresponsible' through the destructive consent that is associated with the absence of responsibility.

Box 2 is rooted in a similar level of disinterest in the community but, combined with an increase in the level of independence from the leader, the consequence is a formal 'anarchy' – without leadership – and without the community that supporters of anarchism suggest would automatically flow from the absence of individual leaders. The result is a leader who resembles a 'herder of cats' – an impossible task. We will return to anarchism in the final chapter.

Box 3 – the theocracy – generates that community spirit in buckets but only because the leader is deemed to be a deity, a divine leader whose disciple followers are compelled to obey through religious requirement: the white elephant described above. That consent remains constructive if – and only if – the leader is indeed divine, a god whose omniscience and omnipotence are unquestionably present. However, it is clear that although many charismatics generate cults that would ostensibly sit within this category, the consent often becomes destructive because the leader is in fact a false god, misleading rather than leading his or her disciples.

The final category, Box 4 – the heterarchy – denotes an organization in which the leaders recognize their own limitations, in the fashion of Socrates, and thus leadership is distributed according to the perceived requirements of space and time (a rowing squad is a good example of a heterarchy in which the leadership switches between the cox, the captain, the stroke, and the coach depending on the situation). That recognition of the limits of any individual leader generates a requirement for responsible followers to compensate for these limits, which is best served through constructive dissent, in which followers are willing to dissent from their leader if the latter is deemed to be acting against the interests of the community.

Perhaps an ancient Chinese story, retold by Phil Jackson, coach of the phenomenally successful Chicago Bulls basketball team, makes this point rather more emphatically. In the 3rd century BC, the Chinese Emperor Liu Bang celebrated his consolidation of China with a banquet where he sat surrounded by his nobles and military and political experts. Since Liu Bang was neither noble by birth nor an expert in military or political affairs, one of the guests asked one of the military experts, Chen Cen, why Liu Bang was the emperor. Chen Cen's response was to ask the questioner a question in return: 'What determines the strength of a wheel?' The guest suggested the strength of the spokes, but Chen Cen countered that: 'Two sets of spokes of identical strength did not necessarily make wheels of identical strength. On the contrary, the strength was also affected by the spaces between the spokes, and determining the spaces was the true art of the wheelwright.' Thus, while the spokes represent the collective resources necessary to an organization's success – and the resources that the leader lacks – the spaces represent the autonomy for followers to grow into leaders themselves.

In sum, holding together the diversity of talents necessary for organizational success is what distinguishes a successful from an unsuccessful leader: leaders don't need to be perfect but, on the contrary, they do have to recognize that the limits of their knowledge and power will ultimately doom them to failure unless they rely upon their subordinate leaders and followers to compensate for their own ignorance and impotence. Real white elephants – albinos – do exist, but they are so rare as to be irrelevant for those who are looking for them to drag us out of the organizational mud; far better to find a good wheelwright and start the organizational wheel moving. In effect, leadership is the property and consequence of a community rather than the property and consequence of an individual leader. Moreover, whereas white elephants are born, wheelwrights are made. In fact, the analogy is useful in distinguishing between the learning pedagogies of both, for while those who believe themselves born to rule need no teachers or advisers, but merely supplicant followers, those who are wheelwrights have to serve an apprenticeship in which they are taught how to make the wheel and in which trial and error play a significant role.

Leadership as the god of small things

Another resolution of this paradox is that the focus should be shifted from the leader to leader*ship* – such that, as a social phenomenon, the leadership characteristics may well be present within the leadership team or the followers even if no individual possesses them all. Thus it is the crew of the metaphorical 'ship', not the literal ship's 'captain', that has the requirements to construct and maintain an organization; hence the need to put the 'ship' back into 'the leadership'. In other words, rather than leadership being restricted to the gods, it might instead be associated with the opposite. As Arundhati Roy remarks about her own novel, 'To me the god of small things is the inversion of God. God's a big thing and God's in control.' Here, I want to suggest that leadership is better configured as the 'god of Small Things'.

The Big Idea, then, is that there isn't one; there are only lots of small actions taken by followers that combine to make a difference. This is not the same as saying that small actions operate as 'tipping points', though they might, but rather that big things are the consequence of an accumulation of small things. An organization is not an oil tanker which goes where the captain steers it, but a living and disparate organism, a network of individuals – its direction and speed are thus a consequence of many small decisions and acts. Or, as William Lowndes (1652–1724), Auditor of the Land Revenue under Queen Anne, suggested, 'Take care of the pence and the pounds will take care of themselves.' This has been liberally translated as 'Take care of the small things and the big things will take care of themselves', but the important thing here is to note the shift from individual heroes to multiple heroics. This doesn't mean that CEOs, head teachers, chief constables, army generals, and so on are irrelevant; their roles are critical – as we shall see in the final chapter – indeed, their own preparation for the 'big' decision that may derive from the accumulation of many small acts and decisions.

Another way of putting this is that the traditional focus of many leadership studies – the decision-making actions of individual leaders – is better configured as the consequence of 'sense-making' activities by organizational members. As Weick suggests, what counts as 'reality' is a collective and ongoing accomplishment as people try to make sense of the 'mess of potage' that surrounds them, rather than the consequence of rational decision-making by individual leaders. That is not to say that sense-making is a democratic activity, because there are always some people more involved in sense-making than others, and these 'leaders' are those '*bricoleurs*' – people who make sense from the variegated materials with which they are faced and manage to construct a novel solution to a specific problem from this assembly of materials. Because of this, success and failure are often dependent upon small decisions and small acts – both by leaders, and by 'followers' who also 'lead'. This implies not that we should abandon Plato's question, 'Who should rule us?', but focus more on Popper's question, 'How can we stop our rulers ruining us?' In effect, we cannot secure omniscient leaders, but because we concentrate on the selection mechanism, those who become formal leaders often assume they are omniscient and are therefore very likely to make mistakes that may affect all of us mere followers and undermine our organizations.

Take, for example, the infamous British Vice-Admiral Sir George Tryon whose actions on 22 June 1893 off the coast of Syria caused the loss of his own flagship, the *Victoria*, after he insisted that the British fleet, then split into two columns, turn towards each other in insufficient space. Despite being warned by several subordinates that the operation was impossible, Tryon insisted on its execution and 358 sailors were drowned – including Tryon. At the subsequent courts martial of Rear Admiral Markham on the *Camperdown* that rammed the *Victoria*, he was asked, 'if he knew it was wrong why did he comply?' 'I thought' responded Markham, 'Admiral Tryon must have some trick up his sleeve.' The court found Tryon to blame but accepted that it 'would be fatal for the Navy to encourage subordinates to question superordinates'. Thus, to misquote Burke, it only takes the good follower to do nothing for leadership to fail.

Nor are attributions of omniscience limited to national military or political leaders alone. For example, when the Air Florida 90 ('Palm 90') flight crashed on 13 January 1982 in poor weather conditions, it is apparent from the conversation between Captain Larry Wheaton and the 1st Officer Roger Pettit that the latter was unconvinced that the plane was ready for lift-off, yet his failure to stop Wheaton from going ahead inadvertently led to the crash. Precisely the same thing occurred in the Tenerife air crash where the co-pilot thought that there was a problem but failed to prevent the pilot from taking off in a dangerous situation because his warnings were too 'mitigated' (another plane was taking off directly in front of them and, unbeknown to the co-pilot, his own pilot did not have permission to take off). In fact, the British Royal Air Force has a 'failsafe' mechanism within their Crew Resource Management System which effectively allows any member of a plane's crew – at any rank – to demand the captain abandons the take-off or landing, in the same way that the British Army and Navy have 'stop-fire' systems that allow juniors to override their seniors when live firing is underway and the junior recognizes a danger that their senior cannot see.

Alfred Sloan, president of General Motors, faced a similar problem with his board but was able to recognize the manifestations of destructive consent:

> 'Gentlemen, I take it we are all in complete agreement on the decision here?'
>
> [Consensus of nodding heads.]
>
> 'Then I propose we postpone further discussion of this matter until our next meeting to give ourselves time to develop disagreement and perhaps gain some understanding of what the decision is all about.'

Three hundred years earlier, the Japanese samurai Yamamoto Tsunetomo recalled an equivalent:

> Last year at a great conference there was a certain man who explained his dissenting opinion and said that he was resolved to kill the conference leader if it was not accepted. This motion was passed. After the procedures were over the man said, 'Their assent came quickly. I think that they are too weak and unreliable to be counsellors to the master.'

What can be done about this problem? Clearly the provision of honest and timely advice to leaders – constructive dissent – provides an appropriate solution, but it is equally clear, first that leaders tend to discourage this by recruiting and appointing subordinates who are 'more aligned with the official line' – that usually means sycophants who provide destructive consent. Moreover, leaders' unwillingness to admit to mistakes reinforces followers' attribution of omniscience. Historically, only the royal 'fool', or court jester, could provide constructive dissent and survive, primarily because the advice was wrapped up in humour and therefore could be publicly dismissed by the monarch, even if privately he or she could then reconsider it rather more carefully. There is, perhaps, no better example of the difficulty and importance of this role than the Fool in Shakespeare's *King Lear*.

Lear, having given away his kingdom to his daughters in a show of bravado and omnipotence, is warned first by his loyal follower, Kent, that the action is foolhardy, but Kent is exiled for his honesty. Then the Fool attempts the same advice but does so through a series of riddles that, unfortunately, Lear begins to understand only when it is too late:

> Fool: That lord that counsell'd thee
> To give away thy land,
> Come place him here by me,
> Do thou for him stand:
> The sweet and bitter fool
> Will presently appear;
> The one in motley here,
> The other out there
> Lear: Dost thou call me fool, boy?
> Fool: All thy other titles thou hast given away; that thou wast born with.

> (*King Lear*, Act 1, Scene 1, 154–65)

It is possible to recreate the role of honest advisor played by Shakespeare's Fool without the 'motley' clothes and perhaps with more success, either by leaders relying on one or more individuals whose position cannot be threatened by the advice proffered, and it may also be possible to institutionalize the role by requiring all members of a decision-making body to enact the role of 'devil's advocate' in turn. In this way, the advice is required by the role and not derived from the individual, and hence should provide some degree of protection from leaders annoyed by the 'helpful' but perhaps embarrassing advice of their subordinates.

Nevertheless, the contested nature of charisma – both in terms of its origins and existence – leaves unresolved the yearning for perfection in leaders that perhaps also reflects our collective dissatisfaction with the lives of unacknowledged followers – the gods of small things. As Albert Schweitzer in his autobiography *Out of My Life and Thought* remarked:

> Of all the will toward the ideal in mankind only a small part can manifest itself in public action. All the rest of this force must be content with small and obscure deeds. The sum of these, however, is a thousand times stronger than the acts of those who receive wide public recognition. The latter, compared to the former, are like the foam on the waves of a deep ocean.

This is a critical assault upon the idea that leadership can be reduced to the personality and behaviour of the individual leader and implies that we should recognize that organizational achievements are just that – achievements of the entire organization rather than merely the consequence of a single heroic leader. Yet, although it is collective leaders and collective followers who move the wheel of history along, it is often their formal or more Machiavellian individual leaders who claim the responsibility, leaving most people to sink unacknowledged by history, nameless but not pointless. George Eliot makes this poignantly clear at the end of her novel *Middlemarch* in her description of Dorothea:

> Her full nature, like that river of which Cyrus broke the strength,
> spent itself in channels which had no great name on the earth.
> But the effect of her being on those around her was incalculably
> diffusive: for the growing good of the world is partly dependent on
> unhistoric acts; and that things are not so ill with you and me as they
> might have been, is half owing to the number who lived faithfully
> a hidden life, and rest in unvisited tombs.

Leaders are important – and we shall consider their role in the final chapter – but there are whole rafts of other elements that are also important, and it is often these that make the difference between success and failure. Perhaps the least understood or evaluated of these other elements is the role of the followers, without whom leaders cannot exist. But this does not mean that we can abandon the individual leader and rely upon the spontaneous leadership of the collective – as we shall see in the final chapter.

Chapter 8
Can we do without leaders?

> Cut doors and windows for a room;
> It is the holes which make it useful.
> Therefore profit comes from what is there;
> Usefulness from what is not there.
>
> (*Tao Te Ching*, Verse 11)

In Chapter 7, I suggested that we needed to put the 'ship' back into leadership if we were to understand how leadership actually worked – in effect, we needed to bring the collective back into leadership. But there is an equivalent danger of eliminating leaders from collaborative or distributive leadership to the point where – if we only just collaborated with each other more – we could resolve the world's problems collectively and without recourse to leaders. In this final chapter, I want to suggest that this is as mistaken as the assumption that leaders don't need to think about followers, but in this case I want to put the leader back into leadership.

In an era of global problems – whether they are financial, environmental, religious, social, or political – the calls for post-heroic leadership have come ever thicker. The alternatives to heroic leadership (for there are several varieties) imply that leadership is unnecessary, or that it can be distributed equally amongst the collective, or that once the cause of conflict – whether that is private property, as Marx suggested, or religion – is removed, it becomes unnecessary, or that heroic leadership is the consequence rather than the cause of organization. In attempting to escape from the clutches of heroic leadership, we now seem enthralled by its apparent opposite – distributed leadership: in this post-heroic era we will all be leaders so that none are.

The idea that leadership could be an unnecessary aspect of society or organization, or that it should be 'distributed', either moderately (so that leadership is shared) or radically (so that, because everyone is a leader, no-one is), has long antecedents. In practice, many hunter-gatherer societies – such as the Hadza of Tanzania – operate without a single formal leader, and leadership tasks are distributed so that any individual can 'lead' a hunt or suggest a move to new territory and so on. Many such hunter-gatherer societies adopt formal leadership systems only when coerced by colonizing forces – as did many American Indian tribes, for example. But even those cultures without institutionalized leaders still retain elements of leadership: hence the Comanche, while embodying the most mobile and anti-authoritarian culture of all American Indians, followed temporary leaders when war, hunting, or their religion required. Similarly, the Nuer followed what Evans-Pritchard described as a 'segmentary' system – a mobile mix of family-based groups that would constantly align and realign themselves to other family groups, but without institutional leadership.

Such limited manifestations of leadership are even rarer in the West, and as we have moved from hunter-gatherer societies through the so-called 'warlord era' (roughly from the end of the last ice age to the industrial era), associated with the development of settled agriculture to the large-scale industrial societies, the form of leadership has apparently changed to the point where institutional and administrative forms of democracy and bureaucracy have displaced the warlord with temporary networks of political, business, cultural, and military leaders that many would argue mirrored the alpha-males of the warlord era.

However, in the 21st century, when wicked problems appear to prevail, the world might be better served through collaborative leadership that displaces the 20th-century warlords with a governance system more suited to those who conventionally suffer from the acts of warlords.

The link between warlords (including absolute monarchies and political dictatorships) and their various supportive priesthoods has often been used to defend leadership on the basis of its sacred link with a god of some variety. Whether that link is the 'divine right' of monarchs, or the representation of secular leaders as demi-gods in their own right, or even the attribution of divine status by followers to their leaders, it is clear that leadership has some connection to the realm of the sacred. But how important is the connection, and what does it imply for redistributing authority away from formal and individual leaders?

It might have been thought that the secularization of the West which began with the Enlightenment would have undermined the sacred aspect of leadership through the separation of the state from the church. Nietzsche certainly suggested in *The Gay Science* that the metaphorical death of god might act as a release on humanity, providing the open sea as a canvas upon which to paint new beginnings, so one might conclude that the secularization of society could initiate a new approach to leadership bereft of its adulation of god-like leaders. But Nietzsche had other questions to ask:

> God is dead. God remains dead. And we have killed him. How shall we comfort ourselves, the murderers of all murderers? What was holiest and mightiest of all that the world has yet owned has bled to death under our knives: who will wipe this blood off us? What water is there for us to clean ourselves? What festivals of atonement, what sacred games shall we have to invent? Is not the greatness of this deed too great for us? Must we ourselves not become gods simply to appear worthy of it?

> (1991, section 125)

The return of religious fundamentalism of all varieties has rudely shattered the assumption that the metaphorical god is dead, but for Karl Popper this question could only be answered with another question: if god is dead – then 'Who is in his place?' This reconstruction – or perhaps 'reconsecration' is a better word – of the leader implies that perhaps leadership is inescapably locked into the realm of the sacred, and if it is, does that have implications for a radical redistribution of authority?

The issue appears to be less about the sacred nature of leadership – because if there is a way of living without leadership, then its sacred nature cannot be a pre-requisite for organization – and more about how social life can be coordinated. Yet ironically, the constant refrain in 'alternative' communities is one usually enshrined in the sacred nature of the community or the 'sanctity' of freedom. The form of the sacred may well be transformed and be infinitely open to interpretation – but it remains quintessentially sacred. In effect, the denial that anyone else should have authority over oneself – because that would undermine one's integrity – generates a resistant sanctity in the sacredness of the individual or that of the community. Or, as Jo Freeman (one of the leading American feminists of the 1970s) put it, the consequence of structurelessness is not freedom from structure or authority (patriarchal or any other variety) but a shift from formal to informal structure – with all the potential for tyranny that informal groups and militant sects can muster. Freeman suggested that democratic structuring would be preferable to structurelessness because at least then the structure is more transparent and open to change. But again, the delegation and distribution of authority and the rotation of tasks requires all participants to be willing and able to make significant contributions in terms of time and effort. For some, that effort may be displaced: for instance, Fletcher suggests that the new post-heroic models, despite being ascribed as more feminine models, are still essentially rooted in masculine organizations where collaboration, relationship-building, and humility are regarded as symptoms of weakness not leadership. Indeed, the top echelons of organizations remain predominantly in the hands of men, so that post-heroic models of leadership are simply models of post-heroic heroes.

For some, the issue is not so much 'leadership', but what kind of 'leadership', and in particular those aspects of leadership relevant to the development of distributed leadership in which leadership resides in the collective. Raelin attempts to contrast the distributed or leaderful organization with the traditional organization by suggesting that in leaderful organizations leadership is concurrent and collective rather than serial and individual – lots of people are engaged in it rather than just those in formal positions; that leadership is collaborative rather than controlling; that leadership is compassionate rather than dispassionate; and that this generates a community rather than simply an organization. The apparent consequences of distributive leadership, according to Gronn, are threefold: first, 'concertive action' – or leadership synergy in which the whole of distributive leadership is greater than the sum of its parts; second, the boundaries of leadership become more porous, encouraging many more members of the community to participate in leading their organizations; third, it encourages a reconsideration of what counts as expertise within organizations and expands the degree of knowledge available to the community. In sum, leadership becomes not a property of the formal individual leader, but an emergent property of the group, network, or community.

Without wishing to defend 'heroic leadership', there is a conundrum here: if heroic leaders have been with us for aeons – and have been responsible for most of the tragedies that have befallen the human race since records began – why have we only just recognized their fallibility? And if we have known about their fallibility for as long as they have existed, why has no effective long-term, and large-scale, alternative been developed? In other words, is the hypothetical post-heroic leadership alternative really a viable alternative?

Of course, this may be a very Western representation, and it clearly is the case that notions of leadership and concepts of the sacred are often radically different in different cultures – a topic too broad to be covered in this book. Indeed, what counts as leadership and the sacred in the USA often seems to be markedly different from their equivalents in the UK. Satirizing, nay lampooning, religious leaders may be *de rigueur* in many North European societies, but it obviously is not in either Iran or the USA. My concern, then, is not to suggest that either Western or British accounts of the link between the sacred and leadership are valid everywhere, but that there probably is a significant link between the two phenomena in different cultures, though the specific nature of the concepts and the links may be dramatically different across the globe. I will also suggest that the sacred is less the elephant in the room – the thing which dare not be mentioned – and more the room itself – the space within which leadership works. That is one reason why it is seldom raised – because it forms the framework within which leadership works.

The etymology of the term 'sacred' offers clues as to its nature without providing an explanation for it (*Collins English Dictionary*, 2005; *Oxford Dictionary of English Etymology*, 1966). 'Sacred' comes from the Latin *sacer* meaning 'sacred or holy or untouchable', which itself came from the Latin *sancire* – 'consecrate, dedicated to a religious purpose, reverenced as holy, secured against violation; to set apart'. Thus one element of the sacred lies in the distance or difference between the sacred and the profane. 'Sacrilege' – which comes from a Latin compound meaning 'to steal holy things' – transcends this boundary and pollutes the sacred. Indeed, the original meaning of 'hierarchy' was 'holy sovereignty': *arkhos* means 'sovereignty or ruler' and *hierós* means 'holy or divine' in the original Greek. *Hierarkhía* was a sacral ranking, and thus the concept of 'hierarchy' is the sacred organizational space that facilitates god's (or the priesthood's) leadership. The Latin *sacerdos* means 'priest', and 'sacrifice' is derived from a Latin compound meaning 'to make holy', thus a second element of the sacred relates to the essential issue of sacrifice by those deemed closest to god – the priesthood: sacrifice is what makes something sacred – it performs leadership. Finally, 'sacred' refers to 'an attitude of reverence or awe', 'a silence in the presence of the divine'. That silence seems to imply a silencing of the fears of believers as their god, or their god's representatives, displace any existential anxieties, or in the Ancient Greek version, where the gods themselves played out the existential fears of mere mortals.

The etymology, then, suggests that the sacred aspect of leadership involves at least three qualities that pertain to the debate about leadership: 'setting apart' – the division between the holy and the profane; 'sacrifice' – the act that makes something holy; and 'silencing' by the religious or secular leaders of both followers' fears and their dissent. Let us proceed briefly through this sacred grove of leadership before considering whether the sacred aspect is necessary and whether this has implications for working without leaders.

Separation

There is a long historical association between separation, proximity, and leadership. Take, for instance, the 'little touch of Harry in the night' that settles the English army of Shakespeare's *Henry V* on the eve of Agincourt: this is considered significant precisely because followers so rarely get close to their leaders, let alone touch them. Monarchs, of course, commonly legitimated their rule through their links with god, and were therefore only responsible to god, so the assumption that their touch was sacred followed logically from the assumption that their whole being was sacred. These differences – the separation between the profane and the sacred – must be protected through monitoring of the boundary, and this may be achieved through preventing direct or unmediated access to the leader, or by the leader displaying specific clothing or other signs of difference. Of course, different cultures embody different distancing mechanisms, indeed different notions of acceptable distance, but some distancing – whether symbolic or material, and whether we are looking at task-oriented or people-oriented leadership – appears universal. For example, Hitler was noted for the plainness of his uniform, which differentiated him from other Nazi leaders in their heavily bemedalled and ostentatious clothes, but connected him to the 'common people' – though he could never be 'one of them'.

The idea that leadership involves some mechanism of 'distance' between leader and follower is commonplace, especially the belief that proximate leaders are significantly better than distant leaders. In contrast, Machiavelli was keen to note that distance was a useful device for preventing followers from perceiving the 'warts-and-all' nature of leaders, for:

> men in general judge more by their eyes than their hands; for everyone can see but few can feel. Everyone sees what you seem to be, few touch upon what you are, and those few dare not to contradict the opinion of the many who have the majesty of the state to defend them.

This has profound implications for those seeking to become leaders because the ability to control distance, especially to keep others at bay and yourself beyond their gaze, is critical to maintaining the mystique of leadership – as the Wizard of Oz found to his cost after the veil hiding his 'ordinary' nature was drawn away.

Distancing is also a device for facilitating the execution both of distasteful but necessary tasks by leaders and of generating the space to see the patterns that are all but invisible when very close to followers or the action – an issue Heifetz and Linsky capture well with their metaphor of 'getting on the balcony' to see the patterns created by the (organization's) dancers.

While distancing may have been critical to leadership in previous times, the contemporary move in Western democracies, under the glare of 24-hour mass media at least, is to generate an image of leadership that minimizes social distance – hence Tony Blair would speak to the media outside his official residence in Downing Street wearing a pullover and holding a mug of tea – as if he were 'one of us' – though few of us would do that in front of the world's press, and even fewer would call him 'Tony' to his face, whether we were friend or foe.

Nevertheless, Collinson suggests that the over-concentration on charismatic leaders overlooks the possibility that distance also provides significant opportunities for followers to 'construct alternative, more oppositional identities and workplace counter-cultures that express scepticism about leaders and their distance from followers'. This is particularly apparent in the way that humour is used to distance followers from leaders, though again that can also encourage followers to acquiesce to the leadership of their leaders by a functional venting of their frustration rather than organizing their resistance.

The separation of leaders and followers also throws into stark relief the nature of inequality that underpins leadership, despite all the obfuscation about empowerment, distributed, democratic, or participative leadership. Indeed, Harter and colleagues suggest that this inegalitarianism is both legitimate and necessary, generating mutually beneficial inequality – providing certain safeguards are maintained. That the inequality at the heart of leadership *needs* to be legitimated – while equality is often regarded as legitimate in and through itself – might also explain why we seem to have a sacred regard for leadership – because it has to be treated as sacred to maintain its legitimacy.

This might also account for the degree of violence used against those with the temerity to challenge leadership overtly considered sacred, for the sacred can only be maintained if those who act to abuse it – those who commit sacrilege – are severely treated. Hence the gruesome execution meted out to the would-be regicide Damiens as recounted at the beginning of Foucault's book *Discipline and Punish*. Sacrilege – the transcendence of the separation of the sacred from the profane; indeed, the pollution of the sacred – plays a critical role in the construction of leadership as well as being perceived as an assault upon it. For instance, Gorbachev's criticisms of the Soviet Communist Party – his sacrilege – opened the floodgates that eventually sank the Soviet Union. Until his very public verbal assaults, few had dared to speak ill of the Party, but once he had given permission for others to engage in critique the Communist Party's sacred integrity was irretrievably damaged. The same might be said of Tony Blair, whose denunciation of Clause IV (common ownership of the means of production, distribution, and exchange) in the Labour Party Conference of 1994 began the process of transforming the Labour Party to New Labour.

So a critical aspect of the sacred is that it necessarily involves a division between the sacred and the profane; there must be a distance between the two for the division to make sense, though of course the precise nature of the division is very flexible and likely to vary with different cultures. In fact, 'difference', rather than 'distance', might be a better way of comprehending the importance of distinction here. The physical or symbolic distance between leader and led may be great or small, but the difference between the two might be the key to success. In other words, might it be that where difference is removed, so that there are no leaders because all – or none – are leaders, there is no leadership? This is not to suggest that some organizational forms under certain circumstances cannot persist without leadership, but rather that leadership cannot survive without difference. Difference is a performative element of leadership, not a trivial embellishment of status.

Sacrifice

The use of sacrifice in ancient societies is, of course, as commonplace as it is offensive to many contemporary eyes. While the Aztecs were sacrificing hundreds to their sun god and wearing the skins of their victims, Romans, Ancient Greeks, Celts, Carthaginians, Africans, Asians, and seemingly everyone else, were similarly soaked in human and animal blood to appease their gods, to protect the tribe, to ensure fertility or food supplies, to ensure the dominant tribe did not devastate your land or just to ensure your subjugated followers were kept in line. The Ancient Greek tradition of the *pharmakos* involved the ritualized scapegoating – expulsion or perhaps execution – of human victims by a community under threat from war or famine.

Scapegoating

The ritual necessity of scapegoating forms an essential core of René Girard's work and relates to the role of mimesis – the desire of all humans to imitate each other. This appropriation of others eventually leads to expropriation of others, an inevitable rivalry, an aggressive response, and a consequential generalized social violence. Girard suggests that across thousands of years, humans have managed to contain this 'natural' propensity to social violence by the sacrifice of individuals. In effect, the primal murder of scapegoats cleanses the community of greater social violence and generates a temporary peace – until the next cycle of mimetic rivalry and violent contagion required the next scapegoat. Thus the only solution to the Hobbesian 'war of all against all' was to narrow the focus down to the 'war of all against one'. And Kristeva is surely right, very often it is women who are sacrificed to maintain the leadership of men – as so-called 'honour killings', for example, usually imply. Often, of course, the sacrificer becomes the sacrificed, most notably if we think of monarchs, such as Charles I of England and Louis XVI of France, but also some leaders whose very policy had been to overthrow such people – for example, Robespierre, or even Cromwell, who died of natural causes but was then disinterred and his body hung in chains while his head was displayed on a pole outside Westminster.

But we do not need to restrict ourselves to physical death to admit that sacrifice still plays a prominent part in leadership, especially in scapegoating of leaders or followers: democratic regimes frequently scapegoat their political leaders for policy failures, and CEOs frequently scapegoat a section of their own workforce when problems emerge or they themselves are scapegoated by the shareholders. Scapegoats that escape the ultimate sacrifice have traditionally been exiled, shunned, tarred and feathered, had their heads shorn, been demoted, sacked, or imprisoned, and many of these actions have been preceded by a show trial of some form, so that the sacrifice encompasses the widest possible public arena: the sacrifice must not just be done but be seen to be done. Again, non-blood sacrifice may also be the self-sacrifice of the leader. For example, Ford's CEO in 2009, Alan Mulally, promised to run Ford for $1 a year if Congress would provide a financial bailout in 2009.

Of course, we all make sacrifices all the time – we sacrifice a lunch break to clear the email backlog, we sacrifice a lie-in on Sunday morning to get the grass cut, and so on, but the kind of sacrifice I am referring to here is for the collective good – however that is defined. Thus our mundane personal sacrifices that do not involve any effect upon the relationship between leaders and followers are not included in this category. Forgoing a cream cake for the good of your health is not the same as sacrificing the baker to improve collective morale in the bakery. And sacrifice is not an unfortunate and embarrassing aspect of some immoral or psychopathic dictator, but an essential mechanism for the performance of all forms of leadership. Sacrifice constructs the sacred space without which leadership cannot occur.

Silence

The sacred aspect of silence involves several principles beyond that of providing space for reflection: the silencing of opposition and the silencing of anxiety. The former is a role that is well documented (for example, by Collinson and Ackroyd, listed in the further reading section) and need not delay us here.

In principle, the notion that leadership is related to the sacred runs directly counter to existentialism, which operates from the opposite end of the philosophical spectrum: we are not the result of god's plan but our own conscious free acts. However, this approach implies that the anxiety generated by the uncertainty and purposelessness of existence is precisely why the burden of responsibility is so great. Were we to believe in fate ordained by a god, then the burden of responsibility is lifted from our shoulders, since all that we do is already inscribed by whichever god is purported to be responsible. But if all that we do is a result of free will floating without moral precept derived from god, then we appear to be both responsible for our decisions and cast adrift from any foundational moral compass with which to make these decisions. Absoluteness and absolution are the twin promises of this fabled leadership land and this double Faustian pact. For leaders, the pact exchanges privilege and power now in exchange for sacrifice later; for followers, the pact secures a security blanket against 'bad faith' – Jean-Paul Sartre's 'exposure of freedom' that underlies even the most desperate decision between two alternative evils. In effect, leadership silences the anxiety of followers.

Erich Fromm suggested that the fear of freedom was also an essential explanation for our almost compulsive submission to authority. For Fromm, modernity had uprooted people from communal relationships with others, and it was this intolerable loneliness and consequent weight of responsibility that drove us to

20. The dilemma of freedom

seek solace in the protective arms of authority – leaders who were fascist or democratic – for only that way could we avoid the fear generated by personal responsibility.

Where does this leave leadership? On the one hand, we can do without leaders if we want to organize social life through very small-scale and temporary networks, but anything larger or longer-lived seems to require some form of institutionalized leadership. The good news is that we now need to concentrate on mechanisms for holding such individual and collective leaders accountable and on creating a more responsible citizenship that is more willing to engage in acts of leadership. The bad news is that the assumption that somehow collaborative leadership is not as open to manipulation and corruption as individual leadership is highly suspect. We cannot achieve coordinated responses to collective wicked problems simply by turning our backs upon individual leadership – even collaborative leadership requires individuals to make the first move, to assume responsibility, and to mobilize the collective leadership. In effect, the members of the collective must authorize each other to lead because collectives are notoriously poor at decision-making. Leadership is not, then, the elephant in the room that many would rather not face up to; it is the room itself – which we cannot do without. This, in another world, is what Bauman calls, 'the unbearable silence of responsibility'. And this is our collective and individual challenge.

References and further reading

Chapter 1

An extended discussion of some the ideas in this chapter can be found in my *Leadership: Limits and Possibilities* (Basingstoke: Palgrave/ Macmillan, 2005).

M. Alvesson and S. Sveningsson, 'Managers Doing Leadership: The Extraordinarization of the Mundane', *Human Relations*, 56(12) (2003): 1435–59.

J. S. Chhokar, F. C. Brodbeck, and R. J. House (eds.), *Culture and Leadership Across the World: The GLOBE Book of In-Depth Studies of 25 Societies* (London: Psychology Press, 2007).

W. B. Gallie, 'Essentially Contested Concepts', *Proceedings of the Aristotelian Society*, 56 (1955–6): 167–98.

R. A. Heifetz and M. Linsky, *Leadership on the Line* (Cambridge, MA: Harvard University Press, 2002).

P. Rosenzweig, *The Halo Effect* (London: Simon & Schuster, 2007).

K. E. Weick, *Making Sense of the Organization* (Oxford: Blackwell, 2001).

Chapter 2

An extended version of the ideas in this chapter can be found in my article 'Wicked Problems and Clumsy Solutions', in *Clinical Leader* 1:2.

M. Douglas, *Natural Symbols* (London: Routledge, 2003).

M. Douglas, *Purity and Danger* (London: Routledge, 2008).

A. Etzioni, *Modern Organizations* (London: Prentice Hall, 1964).

A. Jones, *The Innovation Acid Test* (London: Triarchy Press, 2008).

S. Milgram, *Obedience to Authority: An Experimental View*, 2nd edn. (London: Printer and Martin, 2005).

H. Rittell and M. Webber, 'Dilemmas in a General Theory of Planning', *Policy Sciences*, 4 (1973): 155–69.

M. Stein, 'The Critical Period of Disasters: Insights from Sensemaking and Psychoanalytic Theory', *Human Relations*, 57(10) (2004): 1243–61.

M. Sternin, J. Sternin, D. Marsh, and A. Rapid, 'Sustained Childhood Malnutrition Alleviation Through a "Positive Deviance" Approach in Rural Vietnam: Preliminary Findings', in *Health Nutrition Model: Applications in Haiti, Vietnam and Bangladesh*, ed. O. Wollinka, E. Keeley, B. R. Burkhatler, and N. Bashir (Arlington, VA: Basic Books, 1997).

M. Verweij and M. Thompson (eds.), *Clumsy Solutions for a Complex World: Governance, Politics and Plural Perception* (Basingstoke: Palgrave/Macmillan, 2006).

P. G. Zimbardo, *The Lucifer Effect: How Good People Turn Evil* (London: Rider, 2009).

Chapter 3

An extended version of some of the ideas in this paper can be found in 'Leadership, 1965–2006: Forward to the Past or Back to the Future?', in *Mapping Management Studies*, ed. S. Dopson and M. Earl (Oxford: Oxford University Press, 2007).

L. H. Keeley, *War Before Civilization: The Myth of the Peaceful Savage* (Oxford: Oxford University Press, 1996).

D. McGregor, *The Human Side of Enterprise* (New York: McGraw-Hill, 1960).

A. Maslow, 'A Theory of Human Motivation', *Psychological Review*, 50 (1943): 370–96.

T. Peters and R. H. Waterman, *In Search of Excellence* (London: Harper and Row, 1982).

Chapter 4

C. Boehm, *Hierarchy in the Forest* (Boston: Harvard University Press, 2001).

L. L. Carli and A. H. Eagly, 'Gender and Leadership', in *The Sage Handbook of Leadership*, ed. A. Bryman, D. Collinson, K. Grint, B. Jackson, and M. Uhl Bien (London: Sage, 2011).

T. Carlyle, *On Heroes, Hero Worship and the Heroic in History* (London: Echo Library, 2007).

K. Grint, *Leadership: Limits and Possibilities* (Basingstoke: Palgrave/Macmillan, 2005).

G. Knopp, *Hitler's Children* (London: Sutton, 2002).

D. Lewis, *The Man Who Invented Hitler* (London: Headline Books, 2004).

N. Nicholson, *Managing the Human Animal* (London: Texere Publishing, 2003).

G. Sheffield, *Leadership in the Trenches* (Basingstoke: Macmillan, 2000).

F. De Waal, *Chimpanzee Politics: Power and Sex Among Apes* (Baltimore: Johns Hopkins University Press, 2000).

L. S. Warner and K. Grint, 'American-Indian Ways of Leading and Knowing', *Leadership*, 2(2) (2006): 225–44.

E. Wenger, *Communities of Practice: Learning, Meaning, and Identity* (Cambridge: Cambridge University Press, 1999).

Chapter 5

M. Alvesson and Y. D. Billing, *Understanding Gender and Organizations* (London: Sage, 1997).

B. Anderson, *Imagined Communities* (London: Verso, 1983).

P. Backé, 'The Role of Fashion "Supermodels" in Advertising', unpublished D.Phil, Oxford University, 2000.

M. Gladwell, *Blink* (London: Penguin, 2006).

M. A. Hogg and D. J. Terry, *Social Identity Processes in Organizational Contexts* (London: Psychology Press, 2002).

S. M. Kaplan, M. M. Klebanov, and M. Sorensen, 'Which CEO Characteristics and Abilities Matter?', Swedish Institute for Financial Research, Conference on the Economics of the Private Equity Market; AFA, 2008, New Orleans Meetings Paper. Available at SSRN: <http://ssrn.com/abstract=972446> accessed 6 April 2010.

N. Keohane, 'On Leadership', *Perspectives on Leadership*, 3(4) (2005): 705–22.

I. Pears, 'The Gentleman and the Hero: Wellington and Napoleon in the Nineteenth Century', in *Leadership: Classical, Contemporary and Critical Approaches*, ed. K. Grint (Oxford: Oxford University Press, 1997).

N. Smith, V. Smith, and M. Verner, 'Do Women in Top Management Affect Firm Performance? A Panel Study of 2500 Danish Firms', Institute for the Study of Labour, Bonn, Discussion Paper 1708 (2005).

Chapter 6

B. M. Bass, *Leadership and Performance Beyond Expectations* (New York: Free Press, 1985).

R. R. Blake and J. S. Mouton, *The Managerial Grid* (Houston: Gulf, 1964).

J. Bratton, K. Grint, and D. Nelson, *Organizational Leadership* (Mason, OH: Thomson-South-Western, 2005).

J. MacGregor Burns, *Leadership* (New York: Harper and Row, 1978).

R. Cowsill and K. Grint, 'Leadership, Task and Relationship: Orpheus, Prometheus and Janus', *Human Resource Management Journal*, 18(2) (2008): 188–95.

R. J. House, 'A Path–Goal Theory of Leader Effectiveness', *Administrative Science Quarterly*, 16 (1971): 321–38.

J. M. Howell, 'Two Faces of Charisma: Socialized and Personalized Leadership in Organizations', in *Charismatic Leadership: The Elusive Factor in Organizational Effectiveness*, ed. J. A. Conger and R. N. Kanungo (San Francisco: Jossey-Bass, 1988).

B. Jackson and K. Parry, *A Very Short, Fairly Interesting and Reasonably Cheap Book about Studying Leadership* (London: Sage, 2007).

M. Weber, *Economy and Society* (Berkeley: University of California Press, 1978).

A. Zaleznik, 'Charismatic and Consensus Leaders: A Psychological Comparison', *Bulletin of the Meninger Clinic*, 38 (1974): 22–38.

Chapter 7

K. Grint, *Leadership: Limits and Possibilities* (Basingstoke: Palgrave/ Macmillan, 2005).

B. Kellerman, *How Followers Are Creating Change and Changing Leaders* (Boston: Harvard Business School Press, 2008).

R. E. Riggio, I. Chaleff, and J. Lipman-Blumen, *The Art of Followership: How Great Followers Create Great Leaders and Organizations* (San Francisco: Jossey Bass, 2008).

Chapter 8

Some of the ideas in this chapter are covered at greater length in my article 'Leadership and the Sacred', *Organization Studies* (2010): 89–107.

Z. Bauman, *Postmodern Ethics* (Oxford: Blackwell, 1993).

D. D. Chrislip and C. E. Larson, *Collaborative Leadership: How Citizens and Civic Leaders Can Make a Difference* (San Francisco: John Wiley, 1994).

D. Collinson, 'Questions of Distance', *Leadership*, 1(2) (2005): 235–50.

D. Collinson and S. Ackroyd, 'Resistance, Misbehaviour and Dissent', in *The Oxford Handbook of Work and Organization*, ed. S. Ackroyd, P. Thompson, R. Batt, and P. Tolbert (Oxford: Oxford University Press, 2005).

W. Draft, *The Deep Blue Sea* (San Francisco: Jossey Bass, 2001).

E. E. Evans-Pritchard, *The Nuer* (Oxford: Oxford University Press, 1940).

J. K. Fletcher, 'The Paradox of Post-Heroic Leadership: An Essay on Gender, Power and Transformational Change', *Human Relations*, 15(5) (2004): 647–61

M. Foucault, *Discipline and Punish* (Harmondsworth: Penguin, 1991).

J. Freeman, 'The Tyranny of Structurelessness', *Berkeley Journal of Sociology*, 17 (1970): 1972–3.

P. Froese, *The Plot to Kill God: Findings from the Soviet Experiment in Secularization* (Berkeley: University of California Press, 2008).

E. Fromm, *The Fear of Freedom* (London: Routledge, 2001).

G. Gemmil and J. Oakley, 'Leadership: An Alienating Social Myth?', in *Leadership: Classical, Contemporary and Critical Approaches*, ed. K. Grint (Oxford: Oxford University Press, 1997).

R. Girard, *Violence and the Sacred* (Baltimore: Johns Hopkins University Press, 1972).

P. Gronn, *The New Work of Educational Leaders* (London: Sage, 2003).

N. Harter, F. J. Ziolkowski, and S. Wyatt, 'Leadership and Inequality', *Leadership*, 2(3) (2006): 75–94.

R. A. Heifetz and M. Linsky, *Leadership on the Line* (Cambridge, MA: Harvard University Press, 2002).

J. Kristeva, 'Logics of the Sacred and Revolt', in *After the Revolution: On Kristeva*, ed. J. Lechte and M. Zournasi (Sydney: Artspace, 1998).

N. Machiavelli, *The Prince* (Oxford: Oxford University Press, 1998).

F. Nietzsche, *The Gay Science* (London: Random House, 1991).

A. J. Polan, *Lenin and the End of Politics* (San Diego: University of California Press, 1984).

J. Raelin, *Creating Leaderful Organizations: How to Bring Out Leadership in Everyone* (San Francisco: Berrett-Koehler, 2003).

Sartre, J.-P., *Existentialism and Humanism* (London: Methuen, 1973).

L. S. Warner and K. Grint, 'American-Indian Ways of Leading and Knowing', *Leadership*, 2(2) (2006): 225–44.

Glossary

authority: legitimate power

bad faith: Jean-Paul Sartre's term for decision-making that denies responsibility

bricoleur: a do-it-yourself pragmatic experimenter

calculative compliance: Etzioni's term for compliance rooted in rational behaviour

charisma (strong): Weber's original term for the supernaturally gifted individuals destined to save us in crises

charisma (weak): the subsequent watering down of Weber's original sense to imply strong character

clumsy solutions: an approach to problem-solving rooted in transgressing elegant cultural boundaries

coercive compliance: Etzioni's term for compliance rooted in force

command: a decision-style associated with crisis

community of fate: a community bound together by a shared fate

community of practice: Wenger's original model of learning rooted in collective practice not individual cognition

competence: a discrete skill or trait

concertive action: distributive leadership whereby the whole is greater than the sum of the parts

constructive dissent: a form of follower dissent intended to protect the collective and prevent leaders from taking erroneous decisions

contingency theory: a model of leadership that relates an understanding of the situation to a form of leadership behaviour

cosmology episode: a critical point in a situation that threatens the sense-making of the individuals involved

critical problems: a problem defined by the commander as a crisis

destructive consent: a form of follower assent that threatens the collective by acquiescing to an erroneous decision by its leaders

devil effect: the assumption that a bad first impression (dis)colours all subsequent impressions

distancing: a mechanism by which leaders and followers keep each other apart physically and/or symbolically

distributed leadership: a form of collective leadership

egalitarianism: a political and cultural model rooted in equality and shared decision-making

elegant solutions: solutions that appear consistent with the cultural environment from which they appear

empathy: the ability to see the world through somebody else's eyes

essentially contested concept: Gallie's original term for a concept that would remain without consensus

fatalism: a cultural approach whereby resignation and acquiescence prevail

fatalist community: a community that has collectively given up its ability to resist or change

golden bridge: Sun Tzu's term for the device that enables 'the other' to save face and avoid further conflict

Great Man theory: Carlyle's original model for explaining the development of history through the actions of a tiny number of extraordinary men

grid/group: Douglas's terms for constructing her cultural heuristic

halo effect: the assumption that a first positive impression colours all aspects of 'the other'

hard wiring: the assumption that behaviours are genetically coded into humans and therefore beyond change

heterarchy: a mobile hierarchy in which decision-making changes with the situation

hierarchy: a model of organizational coordination and decision-making in which inequalities of power and knowledge increase with ascendant position

hierarchy of needs: Maslow's original model that suggests that lower (physiological) needs take priority over higher (cognitive) needs

ideal types: Weber's original methodological device for comparing organizational forms by reference to a theoretically perfect (but non-existent) model

individualism: the cultural model that explains the world by reference to individual economically rational action and logical patterns of behaviour

institutional sclerosis: Olsen's claim that over time organizations became more rigid and inefficient

inverse learning: the assumption that learning to lead derives from responding to cues from followers

irresponsible followership: a model of followership that attributes all responsibility for all decisions to the leadership

leaderful organizations: the claim that organizations can have multiple leaders rather than either being led by a leader or being leaderless

leadership: the art of engaging a group or community into facing its wicked problems

LMX: leader–member exchange theory

Machiavellian: a model of behaviour that implies leaders should do whatever is necessary to achieve the public good

management: the science of directing the appropriate process to solve tame problems

mundane activities: the assumption that leadership is actually rooted in the rather humdrum activities of everyday discussions and social exchanges rather than the extraordinary aspects of charismatic leadership

negative capability: Keats's claim that the ability to remain comfortable with uncertainty was extraordinarily important in decision-making

nemo sine vitio est: 'no-one is without fault'

New Public Management: the Thatcher/Reagan/Blair model of public governance rooted in a combination of markets, targets, and customers

normative compliance: Etzioni's term for compliance rooted in followers wanting to follow a leader of their own volition

path–goal theory: House's contingency model of leadership rooted in the relationship between various variables

permission-giving: a model of leadership that suggests that in the absence of formal or informal permission from leaders, followers tend not to take risks

political nous: the ability to read organizational situations

positive deviance: the group of individuals in organizations whose deviation from the rules and norms enables them to achieve what others who comply cannot

power: the ability to get someone to do something they wouldn't otherwise have done

prototypes: a model of leadership that suggests the most likely candidates for leadership are those who embody the most extreme forms of the cultural norms

responsible followers: followers who accept responsibility for the fate of their organization rather than attribute it to the formal leaders

reverse dominance hierarchies: the organizational collection of individuals formed to resist the dominance of an unpopular individual leader

romance of collaborative leadership: the assumption that distributive leadership can solve all organizational problems

romance of leadership: the assumption that organizational success or failure is the direct result of the leader's actions

scapegoating: a form of collective response in times of crisis that allows the collective to remain 'innocent'

scientific management (Taylorism): Taylor's model for increasing the productivity of industry through the application of scientific methods

social capital: the accumulation of social networks that build up effective organizations

social identity theory: a model of leadership rooted in collective identity as the primary source of collective mobilization

tame problems: problems that are commonly solved by the application of standard operating procedures

Theory X: McGregor's original model (close to Hobbes) whereby 'human nature' suggests people are fundamentally lazy and selfish and need to be coerced into productive work

Theory Y: McGregor's original term (close to Rousseau) whereby 'human nature' suggests people are fundamentally responsible and selfless and need to be freed from coercion if they are to engage in productive work

THWαMPs: tall handsome white alpha-males of privilege

traits: patterns of behaviour or personal characteristics

transactional leadership: a model of leadership that takes the exchange process as critical

transformational leadership: a model of leadership that attempts to lift followers beyond their self-interests

wheelwright leadership: a model of leadership whereby success does not relate to the expertise of the individual leader but to the ability of that leader to engage a team of experts

white elephant: a model of leadership whereby only god-like individuals can succeed

wicked problems: problems that are either new or recalcitrant for which there are no apparent answers, and which require collaborative effort to address

zeitgeist: the 'spirit of the times'

Index

LOGIC
A Very Short Introduction
Graham Priest

Logic is often perceived as an esoteric subject, having little
to do with the rest of philosophy, and even less to do with
real life. In this lively and accessible introduction, Graham
Priest shows how wrong this conception is. He explores
the philosophical roots of the subject, explaining how
modern formal logic deals with issues ranging from the
existence of God and the reality of time to paradoxes of
self-reference, change, and probability. Along the way, the
book explains the basic ideas of formal logic in simple,
non-technical terms, as well as the philosophical
pressures to which these have responded. This is a book
for anyone who has ever been puzzled by a piece of
reasoning.

'a delightful and engaging introduction to the basic
concepts of logic. Whilst not shirking the problems, Priest
always manages to keep his discussion accessible and
instructive.'

Adrian Moore, St Hugh's College, Oxford

'an excellent way to whet the appetite for logic. . . . Even
if you read no other book on modern logic but this one,
you will come away with a deeper and broader grasp of
the *raison d'être* for logic.'

Chris Mortensen, University of Adelaide

www.oup.co.uk/isbn/0-19-289320-3

MEDICAL ETHICS
A Very Short Introduction
Tony Hope

Issues in medical ethics are rarely out of the media and it is an area that has particular interest for the general public as well as the medical practitioner. This short and accessible introduction provides an invaluable tool with which to think about the ethical values that lie at the heart of medicine. Tony Hope deals with the thorny moral questions such as euthanasia and the morality of killing, and also explores political questions such as: how should health care resources be distributed fairly?

Each chapter in this book considers different issues including; genetics, modern reproductive technologies, resource allocation, mental health, and medical research.

'...engrossing taster' – **Paul Nettleton, Guardian Life**

http://www.oup.co.uk/isbn/0–19–280282–8

MOLECULES
A Very Short Introduction
Philip Ball

The processes in a single living cell are akin to that of a city teeming with molecular inhabitants that move, communicate, cooperate, and compete. In this Very Short Introduction, Philip Ball uses a non-traditional approach to chemistry, focusing on what chemistry might become during this century, rather than a survey of its past

He explores the role of the molecule in and around us - how, for example, a single fertilized egg can grow into a multi-celled Mozart, what makes spider's silk insoluble in the morning dew, and how this molecular dynamism is being captured in the laboratory, promising to reinvent chemistry as the central creative science of the century.

'Almost no aspect of the exciting advances in molecular research studies at the beginning of the 21st Century has been left untouched and in so doing, Ball has presented an imaginative, personal overview, which is as instructive as it is enjoyable to read.'
Harry Kroto, Chemistry Nobel Laureate 1996

'A lucid account of the way that chemists see the molecular world . . . the text is enriched with many historical and literature references, and is accessible to the reader untrained in chemistry'
THES, 04/01/2002

http://www.oup.co.uk/isbn/0–19–285430–5

ARCHAEOLOGY
A Very Short Introduction
Paul Bahn

This entertaining Very Short Introduction reflects the enduring popularity of archaeology – a subject which appeals as a pastime, career, and academic discipline, encompasses the whole globe, and surveys 2.5 million years. From deserts to jungles, from deep caves to mountain tops, from pebble tools to satellite photographs, from excavation to abstract theory, archaeology interacts with nearly every other discipline in its attempts to reconstruct the past.

'very lively indeed and remarkably perceptive … a quite brilliant and level-headed look at the curious world of archaeology'

Barry Cunliffe, University of Oxford

'It is often said that well-written books are rare in archaeology, but this is a model of good writing for a general audience. The book is full of jokes, but its serious message – that archaeology can be a rich and fascinating subject – it gets across with more panache than any other book I know.'

Simon Denison, editor of *British Archaeology*

www.oup.co.uk/vsi/archaeology